BRAIN GAMES FOR BLOCKED WRITERS

81 TIPS TO GET YOU UNSTUCK

YOON HA LEE

This book is for Joseph Charles Betzwieser, long-suffering husband, loyal pet astrophysicist, and novel-debugger extraordinaire. I love you, and thank you for fixing all the brokedy books!

INTRODUCTION

Sometimes you have a writing project and it just won't go *vroom*. You know what I mean. You're stuck, or you have four chapters and they feel dead on the page, or your characters aren't talking to you.

Some writers have the great good fortune to possess orderly, analytical brains and to be able to logic their way systematically out of these situations.

I am not one of those writers; checklists and logicking have never worked for me. In fact, one of my favorite things to do when "my book is brokedy" (a phrase my husband has learned to dread) is to brainstorm with my husband, an astrophysicist. *He* possesses an orderly, analytical brain, and he analyzes my book problem and tells me what to do to fix it in an orderly, analytical way. I then make him type up the notes and email them to me. I look over the email. And then...I throw out his orderly, analytical plan for how to fix my book and do something completely different.

Irrational, yes. But it works every time!

I want to add that if you *are* orderly and analytical, there's nothing wrong with you. Every writer is different, and the most important thing is that you figure out what works for you and how to do it. But one thing I've noticed is that there are a lot of books that detail sane, logical, systematic approaches to writing, or getting unstuck when trying to write. I haven't had as much luck finding books that include wild tricks to break blocks.

This book is for those of you who get stuck and whose brains are *not* orderly and analytical, and who maybe don't have a pet astrophysicist to bail you out. It's full of eighty-one things to try when the book just won't book. And who knows? Even if none of them work for you, maybe they'll inspire some completely different idea that *does* get you unstuck.

Special bonus tip: If you're *really* stuck, try using a random number generator to pick one of the tricks to try! You can either use a site like random.org, or use two ten-sided dice to roll the tens and ones digits (percentile dice). If you roll too high (e.g. 92), just reroll.

ASIDE: If you have somehow found your way to this book and you are looking for sane, logical, systematic approaches to writing instead, here are some authors to check out: K. M. Weiland (she has great workbooks along with her how-to books), James Scott Bell's craft books, Randy Ingermanson's Snowflake Method for Writing, and Donald Maass's craft books. This is obviously not a comprehensive list, but it should get you started!

1. THE FAKE SCRIPT

Once upon a time, I was working on a novel that was called, variously, *Origami Souls*, *Paper Knives*, *Paper Souls*, *Pentych*, and other things because content management is not my strength. I'd gotten to a point where I was writing long, lush, beautiful passages of description and scene-setting, something I am good at when I feel like putting in the effort. The problem was, those long, lush, beautiful passages of description weren't *moving the story forward*. It was an elaborate writer's version of procrastination, because it *looked* like work—I was adding words! My wordcount was going up!—but *the story wasn't progressing*.

I decided radical measures were called for. First, I dug out a beautiful velvet-covered purple notebook that a friend had given me. (I like purple, what can I say.) I located a pen, although I'd previously been typing.

And then I proceeded to continue my novel in that notebook as though it were a play, writing nothing but the barest of stage directions and lines of dialogue.

Now, I have to clarify something for you. I am not a playwright; I hadn't the faintest clue about playwriting or screenwriting. I didn't know anything about the proper format and just sort of made it up based on, er, the terrible skits we wrote for animal hand puppets back in 4th grade English. (The single line of dialogue I remember: "You meanie, you!" Hardly Shakespeare or Archibald MacLeish.)

The point of this exercise was *not* to generate a play (or goodness knows, a screenplay—if you're trying to break into film/TV, you want a different book).

The point was that I was using description to procrastinate. So I attacked the problem by switching to a format with *minimal description*. Only dialogue, only action described in the barest terms. It forced me to have characters engage with each other and do things to each other rather than endless navel-gazing about beautiful winter scenery, which is okay in a travelogue but less okay if you're writing military fantasy.

I didn't do this throughout the entire manuscript. I did it long enough to break the block. Eventually my characters and plot found momentum of their own, and I was able to (a) "translate" the quasi-play back into prose, and (b) continue the rest of the novel in regular prose.

If you're in a similar fix—spinning your wheels endlessly writing things that don't move the story forward—you might give this a try.

2. TAROT

Some of you have already looked at the word "Tarot" and run away because it's too woo for you. Come back! I promise I'm not here to tell your fortune.

What I've discovered over the past several years of collecting Tarot decks is that they make great brainstorming tools when I get stuck! If you're generally stuck, you can do what people call a one-card draw—shuffle the deck, pull a card, and either use the art imagery or the meaning of the card (this usually comes in a helpful little pamphlet or booklet with most decks these days) to inspire you.

What's more, if you look on the internet, you can find all sorts of Tarot spreads (a series of card draws and their significance) for people and relationships, which I find helpful when I'm stuck with *characters*. The Celtic Cross is a good all-rounder, but Tarot blogs often publish spreads for every situation imaginable.

Besides which, this is a Golden Age for Tarot collectors or devious writers. There is a deck for almost every theme imaginable, in almost every art style imaginable. There are cat Tarots and vampire Tarots and manga Tarots and fanart Tarots (pick your fandom) and inclusive/diverse Tarots and feminist Tarots. There's sure to be a Tarot that matches your style or the mood of your particular project. The great thing is that with the diversity of Tarot art interpretations, you're not stuck with the traditional Rider-Waite deck to get inspiration from the pictures.

BONUS: I've devised two spreads for characters that I will share here, and which you're welcome to use if they're helpful. Or you could always design your own!

Labyrinth spread

3 4 5

2 1 6

9 8 7

> *1 = the character*
> *2 = obstacles*
> *3 = allies*
> *4 = hopes*
> *5 = plans*
> *6 = possibilities*
> *7 = tasks*
> *8 = foundations*
> *9 = key to getting out of the labyrinth (this card is drawn from the bottom of the deck, unlike the other cards)*

Character spread

3 6

2 1 5

4 7

> *1 = the character*
> *2 = their shadow (their flaw, their antagonist, their Jungian shadow...your choice!)*
> *3 = what they want*
> *4 = what they need*
> *5 = crossroads/crisis*
> *6 = how they might fly*
> *7 = how they might fall*

3. CHANGING YOUR TOOLS

Some of us thrive on routines and predictability, and some of us thrive on chaos and variety. You probably already have a sense of which kind you are. If you're in the former category, this one is probably not for you. If you're in the latter, read on.

One of the things I have to do regularly is to switch *how* I write. On the computer, I sometimes write in Scrivener, in Microsoft Word, in a locked blog post window, in TextEdit, in Hundred Words (a janky app I wrote in Swift with help from actual coders). But I also sometimes write on an Alphasmart Neo (an indestructible battery-powered word processor—sadly, they're getting more and more expensive on eBay), on my iPad, in a paper notebook with a fountain pen or a rollerball.

If you've been feeling stuck in a rut, try changing how you write in some way. This is basically the Comic Sans trick—where you switch your writing font to Comic Sans—only it doesn't have to be literally Comic Sans. It can be whatever you want! Recently I wrote a space opera mini-gamebook in a journal that had pastel celestial art printed on the pages, which I found very inspiring. I decorated it with metallic star stickers as I went. Maybe you've always wanted to write in a leather-bound notebook, or you're writing a steampunk adventure and you have just the right gear-motif washi tape to decorate your adventures with. I've just picked up a journal with black pages because I want to try writing in white or gold or neon gel pen. The possibilities are endless!

4. CHOOSE YOUR OWN ADVENTURE!

Maybe you're faced with a plot challenge—do the plucky rebels win this battle or retreat in disarray? Or even the character version of this challenge—does the plucky monster slayer date the were-basilisk or the vampire?

Well, why not both?

What do you mean? you ask. Let me explain. But first, a confession.

I grew up reading not only the Choose Your Own Adventure (CYOA) books that were a staple of my childhood, but also the more complex offshoot known as gamebooks. Some of you may remember series such as Fighting Fantasy, Lone Wolf, and Fabled Lands. Most of them featured a CYOA-style backbone plus a mechanics system, such as basic stats and a combat system and maybe some inventory for lagniappe.

In the past few years, gamebooks have been making a comeback, partly due to a dedicated community, partly due to kids who grew up reading gamebooks becoming adults and having money to buy self-published gamebooks or to back gamebooks on Kickstarter. My own collection is small but treasured.

All this to say, if you're stuck between choices, *do them all*. Try writing in a CYOA-style format and see what happens. Maybe a preference will emerge, or a new possibility that you hadn't considered.

If you haven't come across gamebooks before, here's an example that will give you the idea:

> *Sarai is sitting down to do their trigonometry homework when a glowing dragon flies through their window and lands on their bed.*
>
> *If Sarai asks the dragon for tutoring on cosines, turn to 2.*
>
> *If Sarai picks up their pointy compass and attacks the dragon, turn to 3.*
>
> *If Sarai calls 911, turn to 4.*

5. EXQUISITE CORPSE

There's a party game known as Exquisite Corpse that goes like this: The first person draws part of a picture, then folds it so as to hide most of their contribution. They pass it to the next person, who draws more of the picture based on what they can see. Then they fold it to hide most of *their* contribution, and so on. The end result usually looks like some kind of Frankenstein's monster. You can see some examples at the Museum of Modern Art website.

How does this relate to writing? Well, sometimes you've hit a wall on a scene and you don't know what to do. It would be nice to hand off the project to someone else (I often ask my husband if he'd like to finish my novels for me), but then it isn't your story anymore. (Besides, he always says no.)

However, you can do the next best thing and find an "Exquisite Corpse" prompt for yourself. Pick a *public domain* book—Project Gutenberg is full of great options—and turn to a random page, pick a random paragraph, pick a random sentence or phrase. That's your prompt. Stick it in your story, and go from there for a few hundred words (or more!). The results will probably be absurd, out-of-character, random—but in coming up with them you might be able to figure out what sensible, in-character, logical thing *should* happen instead.

6. JUICY WORDS

I have another confession, which is that I love poetry. My degree is in math, not a profession known for the poetical (although I did once find an anthology of math poetry in Stanford's library system), but there's something about the careful attention to words, especially in short poems, that calls to me.

I keep around some books of poetry, particularly the kind that features unusual words, to help me when I get stuck. In The Fake Script, I talked about getting stuck spinning my wheels writing endless description. The Juicy Words technique is one that I use when I have the opposite problem: I *need* to write description and my gas tank is empty.

When I find myself describing yet another boring, cliché space casino, or a boring, cliché treasure chest, or a boring, cliché sword, I reach for a poetry book and I flip it open to a random poem and I look for a juicy word. Like "crenellate" or "silphium" or "agon." Something unusual, that will spur me to go beyond the boring and the cliché. Nine times out of ten, this jars me out of my rut and I'm able to come up with a better description.

This is a little different from Exquisite Corpse in that no sane poet is going to sue you for using *one word* in the (English?) language. (If it's *their* trademarked made-up word, uh, obviously don't use it.) Often I don't even use the exact word, but I'm inspired to reach for something that isn't so jejune, like the word "jejune."

Your taste in poetry is going to be different from mine. I like Sonya Taaffe and W. S. Merwin and Mike Allen for this, but there are so many options! It doesn't even have to be a book of poetry specifically; it can be any book or thing that serves as a source of juicy words, whether it's a tome on the historiography of the Crusades or poker jargon or the *New York Times* crossword.

7. THE CAT WALKED ACROSS THE KEYBOARD

Some of you who've seen my social media accounts know that I own an extremely cute, photogenic, and problematic catten. My cat's name is Cloud, she's a tortie, and she loves sitting in front of my keyboard when I'm writing or composing music so that I have to type around her catten butt.

Those of you who are fellow cat (or other pet) owners are familiar with the phenomenon of The Cat Walked Across the Keyboard. It happens when you are doing something important, like working on that novel you have due in two weeks. (Not that I would speak from experience.) My husband says I should just close the door but she meows so sadly and then I let her in. My husband also says that I shouldn't let myself be bullied by a small mammal but she's so darn cute.

Anyway, sometimes The Cat Walked Across the Keyboard can be used to your advantage! (No, really.) Take a typical The Cat Walked Across the Keyboard utterance, like *bgrsv*.

Try using this as a *writing constraint*. You're going to write five sentences. The first sentence has to start with a *b*, the second with a *g*, and so on. Sometimes writing to a constraint will shake something loose. After all, they invented sonnets and haiku for a reason.

Again, the point is not that these five sentences necessarily have to make it into your final draft. Having to stick to this structure might break your block. And if good material emerges, so much the better.

8. VIDEO GAME VISION STATEMENT

How many of you play video games? If you play absolutely no video games at all—no Windows Solitaire, no phone games, nothing—then maybe give this one a miss. But otherwise, a lot of us do play games of some sort, even if we wouldn't necessarily call ourselves "hardcore" gamers. Heck, I've done some small pieces of game design and I'm not hardcore anymore because (surprise, surprise) the hours I could be gaming are usually spent on writing. Also my reflexes suck but shh.

You could argue that even the simplest video game has some kind of narrative or theme: Solitaire is about bringing order from chaos; Pong is competition in its purest form. But some games are more narratively minded than others.

If you're having trouble nailing the *big picture* of your novel (or story), and the more usual outlining methods aren't working for you, how about writing a video game vision statement for your novel? Pretend it's a game and that you're selling it to the execs. What would you write in that document?

You might start with the premise, what makes it different from all the other video games in its category (so it's a first person shooter/military, but it's a first person shooter where the hero is a unicorn and zaps people with their horn!), what the player experience (reader experience) will be like, what cool settings the player will visit. Even better, unlike a video game designer, you don't have to worry about polygon counts or RAM requirements!

If you'd like a truly kick-ass example of a video game vision statement, the one for *Planescape: Torment*, a computer RPG from 1999, is available as a free PDF. It's not just a great vision statement, it's an amazing piece of writing brimming with attitude. Of course, you don't need to emulate the in-your-face style if it doesn't suit your book's aesthetic, but it's one example of how to do it.

Wait a second, you protest, I'm writing a shifter romance and I don't see anyone licensing it as a hip new visual novel or *Call of Duty* clone. *You never know.* Besides, sometimes pulling back and thinking of your novel in game terms can be helpful. I always find it useful to remember that The Biggest Boss Fight Should Come Last, rather than being the second confrontation out of five in the book. This is a principle I learned from video games!

9. OPPOSITE DAY

Do you remember "Opposite Day" from when we were kids? Or maybe you, like me, had an "Opposite Grandpa." Mine loved being Opposite Grandpa. When I was a small child, he would smile broadly at me and say (in Korean), "I hate you *this* much," while stretching his arms out as far as they could go to either side. I understood, of course, that that was how much he *loved* me.

Or maybe you're a fan of *Fullmetal Alchemist: Brotherhood*, which features (as you might have figured out) two brothers who are alchemists. The younger brother, Al, is a loyal, trusting cinnamon roll...until that One Episode where he's sulky and acts out.

Opposite Day is useful when you have a character and they're not talking to you (if you're the sort of writer whose characters talk to them) or you're trying to figure out what your character should *do* and the obvious options just aren't working out. Take the obvious option, and write a scene in which your character does the *opposite thing*. No matter how out-of-character it is, or how improbable. Maybe, it turns out, the out-of-character thing is *in* character after all. Or maybe it will inspire you to dig deep and come up with a third, better option.

For example, let's say I have a character who's dutiful and loyal and never, ever steps out of line—what T. Taylor (*7 Figure Fiction*) calls a "Loyal Dog." And the general (or queen, or CEO) to whom Loyal Dog owes their loyalty has been asked to do their Loyal Thing, and it's just not landing for you. It can generate tremendous narrative energy when that Loyal Dog does, in fact, break out of their role and defy the general (queen, CEO)—and now you've got to figure out what's so important that they betrayed the object of their loyalty.

"Opposite Day" is especially handy if you like to write Magnificent Bastard or Chessmaster character types. The only time a Chessmaster should do the Obvious Thing is when the Obvious Thing is a cover for an Unobvious Thing or they're psyching out the opposition. Of course, sometimes the opposite of an Obvious Thing is Another Obvious Thing, but you can't have everything.

10. ROCKS FALL, EVERYONE'S A GHOST!

Have you ever had one of those Bad Writing Days where you seriously consider taking it out on your characters, to whom you are God, and writing the fateful words, "Rocks fall. Everybody dies"? (I'm told this expression comes from when an RPG's gamemaster gets fed up with the players' shenanigans and arbitrarily kills off the players' characters.) I've certainly had my share of Bad Writing Days, and I've often been tempted to write those words.

You might think that everyone dying would sort of be the opposite of helpful when it comes to figuring out what to do next. After all, dead people can't do things—*or can they?*

I have a minor history of writing characters who get shit done while being dead, because I've written a number of ghost or otherwise undead characters. In fact, my first novel, *Ninefox Gambit*, involved a ghost who was a *control freak*. Also, if you're a vampire writer, this applies to you too! I can't be the only person who's been obsessed with vampire novels. (My gateway drug was Laurell K. Hamilton's Anita Blake novels.)

So here's what you do. Drop some rocks and kill off ALL your characters, or if you're feeling nice, just the ones who are causing you problems. (Reminds me of that old Dungeons & Dragons joke about the "vengeful" dungeon master type: "You won't date me? Your character takes 6d6 fireball damage and dies.")

And then, your characters are now ghosts, or vampires, or whatever kind of undead floats your boat. They have brand-new limitations and brand-new trauma along with all the old trauma. What do they do? How do they adapt?

Sometimes yanking out the rug from underneath my characters like this is great for getting them to behave, or (more usefully) misbehave in ways that move the plot forward. It's especially handy when I'm trying to figure out something about the character's core motivations—their compass north when everything else goes to dust.

Like I said, I have written more than one story involving ghost characters. It's fun showing how effective ghosts can be, and how bad it is for the universe when a ghost or undead character gets to take out their traumatic backstory on the other characters for generations on end.

I do have one caveat, which is that my film agent said (lovingly but exasperatedly), "You do know that it's a pain to film ghosts, right? And that you tend to write a lot of ghosts?" So maybe rethink the ghost thing if your ultimate goal is Hollywood. But otherwise, have at it!

11. IN SPAAAAAAACE!

Speaking of adaptation, sometimes it's useful to take a group of characters and dump them in SPAAAAAAACE. If you're a science fiction writer and all your stories take place in space already (most of my stories fall into this category), don't go away yet! I've got something for you too.

Sometimes I get stuck on the *essence* of a character, what makes them *them*, and it helps me to pluck them out of their native setting (a coffeeshop in San Francisco, a bookstore in NYC, a fantasy castle, you name it) and stick them in space to see what essential qualities carry over. The gadgeteer genius character probably loves mucking around in the starship's innards and inventing a new kind of FTL. The gambler probably still gambles. The aggro mercenary lady who attacks everyone on sight probably still attacks everyone on sight.

The point here is not to create a rigorous scientific extrapolation with a one-to-one correspondence between backstory and characteristics in your original setting and backstory and characteristics in space (unless that's what floats your boat). The point is to start thinking about general trends—the *essential qualities* I mentioned above. If you put D'Artagnan from *The Three Musketeers* in space, what is his essential D'Artagnan-ness that would still make him recognizable even in a space opera? He can still have a code of honor in space; he can still be a master duelist in space, if you work the setting right. You get the idea.

And as you may have noticed, it's certainly not necessary for the new setting to be space or a space opera. If your story already *is* a space opera (I have to raise my hand here), then maybe you can strand your characters in a medieval epic, or a magical boarding school, or a coffeeshop in San Francisco. Your imagination's the limit.

12. CARDBOARD CRACK

So, some of you may already be aware that the collectible card game (CCG) Magic: The Gathering is also known as "cardboard crack" because of how expensive rare cards can get. I promise not to lead you down that dark path!

However, for those of you who found "Tarot" too limiting, may I present you with the idea of using *common* CCG cards as story inspiration? I like taking CCG cards I have lying around and making story inspiration decks based on their artwork or card titles. I did this for my cockamamie Asian space opera Machineries of Empire using cards from the Asian-themed CCG Legend of the Five Rings.

This specific trick probably works best if you're working in fantasy, but if you go digging into the dark annals of CCG history, you can find CCGs themed around the Wild West (Doomtown), science fiction (Star of the Guardians), Hong Kong action film/wuxia (Shadowfist), and other genres. Even better (for our purposes, anyway), a lot of older CCGs went bust, but their cards can often be had for a song if you dig around your local game store, or buy them in lots off eBay. I go for the cheap lots, personally, as I'm not in it to win tournaments, but purely to obtain cards for their art.

I should add that if you're lucky and maintain good relationships with folks at your local game store, you might be able to score some free or inexpensive commons. (CCG cards are usually sorted by rarity.) I've often been pleasantly surprised by how many "bad" cards (i.e. ones that aren't powerful in a game context) are graced by really pretty art. I used to collect CCG horse/unicorn/pegasus art and a lot of generous gamer folk, when they saw my binder full of mechanically awful unicorns, would donate one or two of their cards to the cause. I ended up with a bunch of Pearled Unicorns that way.

My caveat here is that art direction in CCGs past and present can be hit or miss. But if you don't mind sorting through a bunch of cards (or actively enjoy it!), you can find some miniature artwork to inspire characters or events or places.

Of course, you don't *need* to do this with physical CCG cards. With an internet connection and Pinterest you can find plenty of great illustrations in any genre. But I'm a tactile person, and something that lives in my computer doesn't feel "real"; I need to be able to touch it. So I offer this to those of you who are also tactile.

13. SPORTS COMMENTARY

I'm a sf/f writer, and I've noticed that there isn't a huge overlap between the sf/f writers of my acquaintance and sports fans. (Maybe I need more friends?) I'm only a casual sports fan myself, at best—I love tennis and once in a while I'll tune in for the Triple Crown. Which is fine! To each their own.

Still, sports and game commentaries can be very useful when it's time to come up with a plot. Now, there are all sorts of books and methods and beat sheets and websites that talk about ways to outline or structure your way to a plot (Randy Ingermanson's Snowflake Method, Joseph Campbell's Hero's Journey, Three-Act Structure, Gwen Hayes's *Romancing the Beat* for category romance, Gail Carriger's *The Heroine's Journey*, the list could go on). There's nothing wrong with these books and methods! If they work for you, keep using them.

But sometimes I get in a rut and I need a plot structure and the books and methods just don't have enough detail for me. To be blunt, I'm *lazy*, and I want a pregenerated plot without stealing from someone else's book plot.

One thing you can do at this point is to steal a "plot" from a sports match or a game match. I'm defining "sports" very broadly here, everything from tennis to League of Legends (e-sports!) to chess. (My friend the tournament chess player informs me chess is *very definitely* a sport, anyway.) Any match in which there's a goal and up-and-down-nail-biting progress toward that goal works for this.

Now, the trick is, you can't turn off your brain entirely, because just as not all books have equally good plots (sorry, it's true!), not all sports matches have equally good "plots." It's up to you, as writer and expert (and sports fan?) to pick a *good match*. You know the ones. When the score seesaws back and forth, or the underdogs are overwhelmed but make a comeback in the bottom of the ninth inning. That kind of *good match*. If you're not sure you know of a match that has that nail-biting quality, find a friend who's a sports fan (again, it doesn't matter *which* sport) and ask them about their favorite match. Trust me, they'll have something for you.

Once you have the match, either watch a recording (YouTube is good for this kind of thing) or find a commentary (written or audio) that explains, if necessary, the high points and the low points. For example, I became interested in chess in 2020, but I am a rank noob at the game. Watching Magnus Carlsen beat someone up (again) doesn't mean a whole lot to me in itself because chess has a steep learning curve. But I can instead pick up a book like Irving Chernev's *Logical Chess* (a gift from my friend the chess player), which has a bunch of chess matches with every single move commented for the beginner, and use that to map out my plot beats. *Here* the enemy team is caught cheating, *there* the quarterback/hero gets a sprained knee or is otherwise knocked out of commission. Ta-da! Instant plot.

14. TRAPPED IN AN ELEVATOR TOGETHER

There's this old trick if you have two characters (or more than two?) who are not talking to you or each other. You trap them in an elevator, maybe a high-tech elevator with a force field to keep them from killing each other if necessary, and you see what happens once they have nothing to do *but* talk. Maybe, if this is a romance or fanfic, smooching happens next. Maybe you turn off that force field and end up with a nail-biter of a combat scene. Maybe they have a heart to heart.

Usually if I can't figure out what a character should be doing in a scene, it's because I've lost sight of what *they* want, what *their* perspective is. Even more so if there are *two* characters and there's supposed to be some spark (enmity, love, envy) or action going on between them, and they're sitting there like lumps.

Here's the thing about an elevator. I've never been trapped in one, but they're pretty boring places. You're either going up, going down, or stuck. There's not much inside to look at. There's not much to listen to unless you count elevator music, which I don't. And besides, that stuff is more prone to drive you nuts than anything else.

It's in the absence of anything else to do that you learn things about people that maybe they want to hide. Maybe he's nervous about his kid's dress rehearsal for the school play. Maybe she's furious at her bodyguard for almost letting her die last night. Maybe they're psyched for the chess match that might make them the new world champion. Let it all spill out.

It doesn't have to be an elevator, of course, and you can even do it within the "reality" or canon of your story. There's a reason "stuck in a cabin with only one bed" is a romance and/or fanfiction trope, if romance is your genre. Maybe, for a medieval war story or historical, they're stuck in a castle under siege. Maybe they're in an escape capsule for a wrecked starship waiting for rescue. Any sort of situation that creates this sort of psychological isolation and concomitant pressure is a great opportunity to get your characters talking about the things they would ordinarily never admit.

15. FIVE HUNDRED YEARS LATER

I once had the surreal experience of reading the first volume of a history of the 19th century that had been published in 1900, largely from a Western (and specifically American) perspective. My mother-in-law had taken me shopping at a used bookstore and I'd picked it up out of curiosity. There was a whole passage about an American ship that had been sunk in war sometime in the 1800s; I don't have the book anymore and can't remember its title or author. The specific ship isn't important. What intrigued me was that the historian claimed that this ship's sinking in the 1800s was such an atrocity that it would never be forgotten.

So, I'm not a historian, but I took AP US History in high school and a raftload of history courses in college (my guiding principle was that I took almost everything in the department that had the word "war" in the title). I'd read Howard Zinn and Paul Johnson and other historians. And I'd never heard of this ship or this atrocity. It had vanished out of living memory. Granted, I'd spent half my childhood in South Korea, so maybe that was it? But my husband Joe, who'd spent his entire childhood in the USA, hadn't heard of this ship either.

I had a related conversation with my husband about notoriety and atrocities due to a (completely fictional) character I have in one series who committed a massacre that was still remembered four hundred years later. I told him that if he hadn't committed the massacre, if that character had just been a superb general, he might well be forgotten. Joe was skeptical, at which point I challenged him to name five generals, competent or otherwise, from the 1600s without resorting to his phone. He couldn't do it. Heck, I couldn't do it either; all my Western Civilization classes ended at 1500! (I guess I'd look at the Thirty Years' War for a start, but that's all I've got, and I'm painfully aware that that's just Europe, due to biases in my education.)

If you're having trouble seeing the big picture with your characters, especially the kind of characters who are involved in an epic quest or struggle, it can sometimes be helpful to step back and ask yourself, What would be remembered about them five hundred years later? Would the record be accurate? What kinds of recordkeeping are there in your world? Will they be remembered kindly or with scorn? Is the truth of how they lived and loved and bled something that the world was witness to, or that they posted about on TikTok, or were their lives private and inscrutable to future generations? What will they do that's writ large into the weave of their world's history?

16. CARTOON EDITION

I was one of many kids who loved the "funnies" in the Sunday newspaper (yes, this was back in the days when households received physical newspapers) and one thing I tried to teach myself was how to draw cartoons and comics.

Uh-oh, you might say, this is going to be about drawing and I can't draw. Fear not! No actual drawing ability is needed for this particular crazypants exercise. In fact, the webcomic *xkcd* features stick figures. If you can draw stick figures, you can do this. (That said, it's clear from the occasional complex drawing in *xkcd* that Randall Munroe has mad expertise in drawing and draftsmanship, *he just chooses not to use it.*)

I want to introduce you to a great trick if you have a scene or a chapter whose plot rhythm just isn't gelling. You don't need to know how to draw anything more complicated than stick figures.

I challenge you, if you're stuck for plot rhythm on a scene or similar chunk of narrative, to write it as a *three-panel gag strip*. You can do it on a clean sheet of paper if you're feeling fancy, or with sticky notes if you're not. Sticky notes—one per panel—are a great cartooning tool! They're affordable, and if you mess one up, you can just replace it with a fresh one. And you can switch up the order or swap out different versions of panel #2 very easily.

Why a three-panel gag strip, even if you're not writing comedy? While I won't deny that creating a 300-page magnum opus of a graphic novel is a lot of work, stripping down a story into three panels—setup/premise (panel #1), development (panel #2), and punch line/conclusion (panel #3)—requires a great deal of skill. The cartoon format stops you from getting distracted by irrelevancies like what the hero had for lunch at the last train stop (colcannon, maybe, or bulgogi tacos?). Even if you're doing a three-panel gag as a brainstorming exercise rather than actually intending to publish your chapter as a cartoon strip, it's helpful to stick to the spareness of the medium as a way of pushing yourself to boil everything down to the most essential elements.

17. THE ZOO

If you have read any fanfiction at all, then you are probably aware that the main thing fandom got out of Philip Pullman's *Golden Compass* trilogy was that daemons are cool and everyone should have one, no matter which universe they came from.

For anyone who's escaped those books, the idea is that everyone has an animal "daemon" who represents their inner self. Children's daemons change shapes as they try on different identities. Once they reach adulthood, their daemons take on a fixed shape.

You see where I'm going with this, right? So some of you are lucky and characters walk into your heads fully-formed like Athena from the brow of Zeus. (I guess the grass is always greener, etc.) I usually have to work to create characters, and I often have a hard time getting to know them until after I've written the rough draft.

One way of "templating" a character is to give them a "daemon" or (if you read/write paranormal romance) a shifter type! Maybe that vain businessman is a peacock. Maybe that seemingly quiet, well-adjusted girl in the corner of the classroom is secretly a shark.

For something like literal shifter romance you probably want to give your character some of the animal's qualities—a tiger shifter might be physically powerful, a gerbil shifter might be small and unprepossessing—but in other genres you can generate some interesting character depth by playing against type.

18. LAWFUL CHAOTIC GOOD EVIL NEUTRAL NEUTRAL

Even people who don't play tabletop roleplaying games (TTRPGs) have often heard of the idea of "alignment," or your moral orientation Dungeons & Dragons-style: paladins are Lawful Good, rampaging villains are Chaotic Evil, and other character types are everything in between.

One of the tricky things about writing an ensemble cast is making sure that you maximize your use of the character space. That is, unless you're going for a very specific aesthetic, you probably shouldn't make *all* your characters in a boarding school story fiery redheaded soccer players, and you probably shouldn't make *all* your characters in a space mercenary story buff monosyllabic berserkers. Not unless you want your readers to have difficulty telling your characters apart! Readers can be notoriously inattentive. I couldn't tell James S. A. Corey's characters Amos and Alex in *The Expanse* from each other until I watched the TV show, solely because both their names have four letters and start with A, even though their personalities are nothing alike!

I use alignment as a tool for keeping characters distinct, especially in an ensemble cast, because I have nostalgic fondness for D&D. But it doesn't have to be alignment. It could be any personality type sorting tool, whether it's Myers-Briggs (I'm an INTP!) or Enneagram or a fictional system that you enjoy like the Houses in George R. R. Martin's A Song of Ice and Fire books. If you're good at creating nuanced characters from the get-go, you might not need this tool; I, personally, need everything to be almost caricature levels of different so I can "see" them clearly, so typing characters helps me tremendously.

Don't forget that many readers are visual and, if possible, it can help to differentiate characters physically as well as psychologically. I can't remember which author said this (maybe Brent Weeks?), but with George R. R. Martin, he said that GRRM doesn't give us a slow-witted 6'3" giant and a slow-witted 6'4" Giant, he gave us Hodor the dim giant and the quick-witted dwarf Tyrion Lannister. GRRM excels at differentiating a large cast by taking advantage of all the ways that people can be different from each other! He probably doesn't use D&D alignment, but that's no reason you shouldn't, if it helps you.

19. TIME TO CHILLAX

My husband complains that I am a workaholic who doesn't know how to take a vacation. In fact, the first thing I do when I pack for a vacation is to figure out how many personal projects I can take with me. The last time I did a "staycation" in a hotel in my city, I brought along gamebooks, a cross stitch project, watercolor supplies...you get the picture. I argue that the only reason *he* doesn't look like a workaholic is that he's convinced his brain that video games are "work." Certainly his six-hour Warframe or Star Sector sessions look like work to me.

When is the last time your characters have gone on a vacation? Science fiction author C. J. Cherryh notoriously likes to put her characters through the wringer such that they never get a respite. I remember reading her Morgaine books and being surprised that her heroes, Morgaine and Vanye, didn't topple over from sleep deprivation, exhaustion, and hunger.

You might not *literally* give your characters a vacation. But there can be some benefit, even in a thriller, to giving them a respite of some sort, perhaps before you twist the screws harder. A fortissimo sounds louder by contrast after a very quiet passage, after all.

Back when I was working *The Vela* for Serial Box (now Realm), I proposed to the writing team (consisting of the excellent Becky Chambers, S. L. Huang, and Rivers Solomon) that we were working on a fairly dystopian allegory about refugees and climate change, *but* I didn't want the story to be all grim all the time. I say this not because I have any mercy for the reader (please, I'm the writer whose daughter teases me relentlessly about putting genocides in all my books) but because those grim moments hit harder if you give the reader moments of grace or humor. It's often useful to consider whether a book will benefit from some ups to go with the downs, tonally.

The other piece of this is that you can often get useful story fodder from considering *what* your character considers a "vacation." My husband thinks hotels are terrible because all he ever wants to do is stay home and play video games. I want to do work, but in nicer surroundings and with room service. My sister wants to lie on the couch and chillax with *The Great British Bake-Off*.

Maybe one character's idea of a vacation is to go out every night to perform slam poetry. Their girlfriend would rather stay at home and watch cooking shows. The cosseted noblewoman might want to sneak out under an assumed identity and participate in masked duels, while her bodyguard secretly longs to spend all day gardening. It's especially hilarious (evil) when characters have vastly conflicting ideas of R&R!

20. SNEAKERS AND OTHER WITNESSES

Sometimes I get stuck on a scene and I can't figure out how to make it go again. Maybe the characters are talking in circles. Maybe I need to reveal a secret and I can't figure out the best way to do it. Maybe my viewpoint character or narrator feels stale.

One way to unstick yourself in this situation is to switch viewpoint characters. And not just a switch to, say, the other character in the room, but to something completely off the wall. Like your character's sneakers. Or the pencil sharpener on their desk. Or their parakeet.

I got the idea for this particular crazypants exercise from a more conventional characterization exercise in an excellent workshop run by writer and editor K. Tempest Bradford. In her version, she handed out photographs of random people and we had to come up with a description of them, which might include not only physical traits and clothing, or perceived gender and profession, but their surroundings. We also had to do it again from the point of view of one of our characters, and see how that changed from our initial descriptions.

When I did this, my initial description was pretty conventional. My second run from the POV of a character who was a soldier and former assassin was boy howdy different! The photo depicted someone sitting on a bench in a well-occupied park. The assassin noticed things like "There are too many witnesses so this is a bad time and place to kill the target" and "great sight lines, so if I shoot them in the head they're a goner." As someone who is a marshmallow in real life, I do not normally think things like this!

The point here is that a different POV, written conscientiously, will force you to notice different things—about the characters, about their surroundings, about the emotions that are or aren't flying. A coffee mug might have some keen observations about how a businessperson always gets jittery right before a confrontation with a rival; a pair of sneakers might know that the young engineer always paces when she's about to make a brilliant breakthrough on a problem. You might not use all this material when you return to the "proper" POV, but the change in perspective is often helpful.

21. SHOPPING LISTS

My husband writes the world's most boring shopping lists, by which I mean not that the things he puts on the lists are boring (Pocky for me, cat food for the cat, potatoes for that spinach saag recipe he wants to try...) but that the lists are just that: lists. Other than his atrocious handwriting, which we joke about in this household, there's nothing that makes his lists special.

Sometimes my lists are boring, too! But sometimes I want to make sure that something I *really really want* (like Pocky) receives some extra emphasis so it doesn't get forgotten. So I write in all caps or I draw stars around the desired item or a giant smiley face to get my husband's attention. (I have some mobility issues, so my husband is generally the one who does the grocery shopping. That said, I'm a flake, so I need to remind *myself* about the Pocky anyway.)

My daughter, who wants to be an artist, takes it one step further. When it's her turn to contribute to the shopping list and add any items she wants purchased for her, she often draws gratuitous dragons. What's a shopping list without a dragon or three, right?

Why not consider what shopping lists your *characters* would come up with, for groceries or otherwise, and how they might change over the course of your story? It can be fun to compare what your characters *want* (or think they want, always an important distinction) to what they *need*. For example: Lonely half-dragon librarian is shopping for (a) more manga in his hoard, (b) coffee that actually keeps him awake during the morning shift, and (c) a way to get that annoyingly attractive card shark to leave him alone. Everyone needs more manga and better coffee (okay, I'm a tea drinker, but same concept), but we all know that the stunning card shark is the person who will fill the hole in our librarian's heart, if the two can just get past each other's defenses.

Turn this around and you could consider what shopping list your *plot* wants. Does your plot want something off-the-rack or characters and situations a bit more off the beaten path? Is your plot shopping at a dollar store or an appointment-only ritzy place for rich people? For example: Death-defying hostage situation is shopping for (a) a hard-bitten renegade FBI agent, (b) her ex-girlfriend biochemist the hostage, and (c) the fanciest hotel in Malaysia so that you, the author, have an excuse to research fancy hotels on the internet. (Or maybe you're able to do it in person!)

And if you want to add dragons (figurative or literal), feel free to do that too!

22. ALL THAT GLITTERS

There's a saying that goes something like "Beware all enterprises that require new clothes." But clothing says a lot about a person, and unless you're writing about nudists (or aliens, or animals, or robots), your characters probably wear it at least some of the time.

I have to admit that I'm the lazy person who spent an entire trilogy writing about people in military uniforms and color-coded factions, because I have approximately zero imagination when it comes to interesting clothes. All the military characters were basically wearing the same thing. (I realized I *really* had a problem when I went to draw the characters and only knew two *haircuts*.)

If you're stuck in a situation where all your main characters have to wear the same clothes so it's hard to distinguish them that way (firefighter gear, cleric robes, power armor) or just want to try something a little different, consider what your character would be if someone turned them into a piece of jewelry or other accoutrement. Would they be a one-of-a-kind Montblanc fountain pen adorned with a real diamond? A ring carved from the heart of a petrified tree and inscribed, on the inside, with a word in a language that only two people speak? A homemade tongue piercing?

23. PLAYERS AND SUITS

If you've ever played any game, you'll know that people have different playstyles. In a tabletop roleplaying game (TTRPG) like Dungeons & Dragons, you might have That Loner Dude who always plays a grim-dark assassin who sells out the party "because it's in character," and the ham who declaims a ten-minute soliloquy every time their character has an action, and the minimalist "roll-player" who eschews acting and just wants to say "I roll to hit." Some people are all about socializing with other players, some people want to unlock all the achievements in an online game, some people are only there because their girlfriend brought them. Richard Bartle's "Hearts, clubs, diamonds, spades: Players who suit MUDs" is an entertaining typology of player types in multiplayer online games; another specific to TTRPGs is Robin Laws' *Robin's Laws of Good Game Mastering*.

I first came to this understanding of personality types as revealed in gaming through TTRPGs. (My shameful confession is that I am a "roll-player" who always plays a fighter, mainly because I just want to hit things, and I can't act. Coming up with character motivations and descriptions is too much like my day job...writing.) But I also learned that personality is constant across games, which was not initially obvious to me, and this came about in two different arenas: fencing and chess.

I fenced for about two years before being temporarily sidelined for health reasons. (I've since resumed!) Early on, I figured that I would be a cowardly, defensive sort of fighter because in my daily life I am that most marshmallowy of people, a sedentary writer. (I realize there are writers who are NOT marshmallows; for example, horror writer Brian Keene used to be an Army sharpshooter! But this is me.)

But the thing about fencing, even electric fencing where you are encased in armor and there's minimal danger, is that it brings out your real fighting self. There's only truth on the piste. When you're in the midst of a bout, even though it's a sport fight and not a real fight to the death, it's easy for your training to fly out the window under pressure and for your reactions to boil down to instinct.

I learned in critique after my first bouts that (a) I never retreat (even when it would be smarter to) and (b) I always attack. I had to be trained to retreat and to fight defensively. (I fenced both foil, where you can get away with attacking, and épée, where you really can't. Sadly, as a middle-aged potato, I lack the physicality necessary for sabre, which is attack-minded, especially against leggy teenagers.) You can't tell just looking at someone; you have to put them in a fight and see what happens.

I would have dismissed this as a fluke except the same tendencies emerged when I started learning chess in 2020. I am not good at chess (still a noob) but the French Defense would never in a million years have occurred to me. The thought of putting up a wall of pawns and then fussing around behind them fills me with horror.

Imagine your characters as gamers, in whatever game appeals to you. (Maybe they already *are*.) Is it obvious what gamer type they are, or do they reveal new facets of themselves in a gaming situation? Consider: The shy, bookish gazelle shifter is a tactical mastermind. The playboy spends all his time in-game flirting with the same non-player character (NPC), as though he's secretly looking for true love. The take-no-prisoners businesswoman plays a flamboyant bard.

Bonus: if you're writing military fiction or any adjacent genres (I write military space opera for adults, among other things), you can use this, in an exaggerated way, to come up with different fighting styles for any generals or tacticians or captains you have lying around. It can be incredibly fun, in a fictional context, to give your generals completely different styles, just as you might give regular characters different personalities or appearances, and pit them against each other.

24. BOOK CLUB

I once was a member of a book club called the LIGO Widows' Club. LIGO (Laser Interferometer Gravitational Observatory) is the scientific collaborative that my husband works for, and back then he was a grad student working at LIGO Hanford (in Washington state) and I was his stay-at-home spouse. The LIGO Widows' Club, with its tongue-in-cheek name, was a book club for LIGO spouses, most of whom were wives due to the skewed gender ratios among gravitational astrophysicists.

As writers and readers, we like to think that everyone reads, or would if they could, although this is not in fact true. What book would your characters bring to a book club? Are they into romantic suspense, or are they that reader who will read anything with a dragon on the cover, like my daughter when she was younger, or are they someone who searches high and low for young adult novels that have no romance in them?

Especially if you're writing speculative fiction, you can use this prompt for worldbuilding as well as character exploration. Granted, you might be writing in a setting where there *are* no books, either because written language hasn't been invented yet, or because books are obsolete and everyone downloads information directly into their brains, or because books are cursed artifacts that everyone burns on discovery. But it's very likely that your characters care about *stories* in some form. And asking what form *storytelling* takes in your world can be illuminating.

Maybe the dominant form of storytelling in your world is ritualized shadow plays with stock characters. Maybe telenovelas are commissioned by the Empress to form the backbone of high culture, and their creators vie for her court's favor. Maybe all education is conveyed by graphic novels—or your hard-bitten spacefaring mercenaries keep a ship's fanfic archive!

25. WEAPON OF CHOICE

Some of you may have grown up, as I did, playing a murder mystery board game called Clue, where you have to determine who the murderer is, what their murder weapon was, and where they killed the unfortunate victim.

This mode of thought isn't only useful to mystery writers. I am that clueless (pun intended) reader who couldn't even solve Three Investigators or Encyclopedia Brown mysteries, and I'm pretty sure those were at the shallow end of the mystery pool. Just as every chess player has their own style, every character does too when it comes to dealing with dangerous situations.

You may be in a situation where it's helpful to decide what your characters' weapons of choice would be. Maybe the former assassin has a signature handgun he totes everywhere, even when it's a dead giveaway as to the killer's identity. Maybe the herbalist's apprentice, driven to the unthinkable, substitutes a poisonous mushroom for an identical-looking regular mushroom in the prince's meal. Maybe the local tyrant, threatened in their throne room and betrayed by their guards, keeps a pair of tame venomous snakes in their bodice for such occasions.

The question of "weapon of choice" often boils down to two separate considerations: what's *available* and the wielder's *personality*. The assassin might be outwitted in a fight because he's been disarmed and he's scrabbling after that beloved handgun when there's a crowbar *right there* he could use to smash his opponent's head in. The herbalist's apprentice might know, like all the local foragers, that these two particular mushrooms are common and easily mistaken for each other, even though the prince is used to relying on his personal taster and has certainly never had to forage for his own meals. The tyrant, for all their faults, may have been an animal lover since childhood, using their position to collect rare and dangerous specimens.

26. FOOD CATALOGUES

I learned how to write interesting food descriptions not from a writing how-to book as such but from Zingerman's catalogues. (Hint: browsing their website is just as good as getting the paper catalogue, if you want to avoid extra physical mail. Obviously, check other gourmet food suppliers' websites for their ad copy!)

One of the cookbooks that I obtained early in my marriage was a guide to things like balsamic vinegar and extra-virgin olive oil from the Zingerman's folks. Charmed by the descriptions of foods that I had *not* grown up eating, I obtained their catalogues and discovered that it is, in fact, possible to write about something as mundane as oatmeal in such a way that it sounds like mouth-watering gourmet food.

Food scenes tell us a lot about characters and their societies because not only is food a basic human need (if you're thinking about Maslow's hierarchy), but because it's also deeply embedded in culture. Is your hero's comfort food a crawfish boil where he can inelegantly but happily slurp out crawfish brains? (I have done this and they are delicious.) Does your character notice if the soup spoon is on the wrong side of the plate? Does she bake gluten-free muffins whenever she's stressed out?

And why stop at food, when you can tell us about the culture and setting with the utensils? I do in fact own sterling silver tableware… but it's a set of eight spoons and *chopsticks*, because I'm Korean-American and it came as a wedding gift from a Korean. Is food served as hunks of dragon-dactyl meat that you have to tear off the bone with your own teeth, or is everything cut up into bite-sized pieces by the chef for the ease of the diners?

There's also the question of where the food comes from. If you're writing a contemporary romance and your characters aren't off the grid, you can usually assume that a supermarket or corner store is close at hand. But if you go into the past or future, food production might become more vexed. If your characters are scientists on a lonely station on a moon with methane seas, where do they get their supplies from? Would they kill for an honest-to-goodness chocolate bar instead of the freeze-dried astronaut food they otherwise have to subsist on? A fantasy setting where even commoners eat meat on a regular basis, as opposed to one where the staple grain is millet and meat is a rarity, tells me a lot about agricultural practices and relative wealth.

27. GREEN THUMB

You know how sometimes talents run in families, and sometimes they skip a generation? My mother has the most amazing green thumb. She keeps a container garden and at one point was busy breeding four-leaf clovers; she got some of the plants to produce five- and even the occasional six-leaf clover as well before she tired of the whole enterprise. She sent my daughter a laminated bookmark featuring a three-leaf, four-leaf, and five-leaf clover as proof of her prowess.

Alas, this is a talent that did *not* transmit itself to the next generation. My sister and I both have black thumbs. In fact, as a sort of family joke, I once gave my sister a bonsai tree...made of copper wire. (It was very fetching—that particular artisan does amazing work.) I told her it was a bonsai she couldn't kill, because I hear all her stories of the parade of plants that come into her hands and don't survive the experience.

What kind of gardeners would your characters be? One might have a green thumb and choose to grow nothing but toxic ornamentals. (I can't help but think of Nathaniel Hawthorne's "Rappaccini's Daughter" here.) Another might disdain anything but herbs and vegetables for immediate use in their cooking. A third might "garden" with sand and stone, Zen-style, perhaps because nothing else is available in a barren land. In a fantasy or science fiction or horror setting, the possibilities are even wilder: fantastic flowers like the symbolic altarskirt roses from N. K. Jemisin's Inheritance trilogy, or alien plants, perhaps with strange intelligences of their own.

Gardening and landscaping choices can also be a way of getting in some extra worldbuilding and telling us about your society's relationship to nature. Is the ideal garden indistinguishable from a slice of the natural wilderness, as with Korean landscaping? Or does your culture prefer mannered hedges and labyrinths? Do your cities make a point of planting trees? Do the houses sport cookie-cutter lawns mandated by the local homeowners' association, or wildflowers that attract native pollinators?

28. PORTRAITS

I used to dread going to art museums as a student, especially when there were rows and rows of dead-eyed portraits of people I didn't care about. Now that I'm taking art lessons, I realize how much skill and artistry went into the portraits that I used to hate.

What's particularly interesting is comparing portraits from different times and places. The Egyptians depicted people partly in profile, partly frontally, because they wanted to show off different body parts from their best angles. Compare this to a Japanese ukiyo-e print or a Renaissance painting or a loving portrait drawn in finger-paint by someone's kid.

I took up drawing because I wanted to know what my characters look like. I have aphantasia, which means that I can't visualize things; for the longest time I thought that people who claimed to "see a movie" when they read a book were pulling my leg. Since I have a limited budget, I decided to learn to draw my own characters rather than endlessly commissioning artists to do their portraits.

But you don't have to draw, or want to draw, to consider what your characters' choice of portraiture or self-portrait says about them. Does she want a soft-focus boudoir photograph to give to her girlfriend? Do they want the painter to emphasize the side of their face that has a nasty scar they picked up in their most famous duel? Does the captive serial killer repeatedly draw himself as a stick figure with his face crossed out?

29. REAL AND IMAGINARY FRIENDS

One thing I have learned from Becca Syme's writing productivity channel The Quitcast, as well as talking to other writers, is that some of us are internally motivated and some of us are externally motivated, and there is nothing wrong with either type. I happen to be internally motivated. While I don't write every day (I am a slow thinker, so occasionally I need to take a few days off to mull things over), I do write pretty consistently.

I have friends who are externally motivated, or who benefit from external motivation. Heck, even I benefit from alpha readers who send "cheerleading" notes (rather than constructive criticism) on my rough drafts. I'm a "vomit drafter" who writes a messy first draft, as opposed to some of my friends who write very clean drafts on the first try. Both are valid styles but have different working requirements.

If you're externally motivated (or even if you're not), it can be helpful to find an accountability partner or alpha reader who will cheer you on as you complete your writing sessions.

But if you can't scare up someone who's willing to send you cheerleading on your daily or weekly snippets, you might be able to *construct* a motivational system. For some of us that's as simple as a sticker chart. I got through most of my first YA novel draft with a sticker chart—it was incredibly motivational to be able to use stickers that a friend from Germany had sent me. Right now I'm doing something similar with a middle grade book, only I'm using washi tape swatches—again, a friend sent me washi tape samples so using them makes me think of her!

The only requirement for a motivational system is that it be something that works for *you*. I have friends who swear by the writing wordcount/habit-building game 4thewords. It might be as simple as that sticker chart, or buying yourself one of those affirmation decks and pulling an affirmation card every time you reach your goal for the day, whether that's to write for two hours, outline or brainstorm for half an hour, or write 750 words.

You might even write daily notes to (and from?) an imaginary friend who thinks that everything you write is amazing. I don't do this exactly, but ever since 3rd grade, I made my little sister read everything I wrote. In the back of my head she's always been "my" audience. Thinking of her encouragement over the years often helps me keep going.

30. KINDERGARTEN TIME!

I remember once reading an extremely long, bonkers fanfic in a fandom that I will not name. (This is not judgment. I have written my share of bonkers fanfic, although I have yet to achieve "long.") One of the wildest bits was when the characters, who were all hardened soldiers, were literally physically regressed to toddlers, complete with daily playtimes and naps, to "heal" them of their emotional trauma. It says something that I can neither remember the author's name nor the title of the fic, but I vividly remember that chapter.

I also once drew a cartoon of some space opera characters of mine as kids in a classroom (great minds think alike?). My friend Sonya commented that it looked like the world's worst kindergarten class. That comment stuck with me too.

As a parent and writer of children's books, I can tell you that the delightful (and sometimes appalling) thing about kids is that they have no filters! My first middle grade book featured a fox spirit who could change her shape. During one of the school visits I did to promote the book, a kid came up to have me sign his copy and asked me, bold as you please, "Are you a furry?" (For the record, I stammered that no, I am not, and he seemed satisfied.)

If you're stuck figuring out your characters' inner desires at whatever point, try regressing them to kindergarten, to an age when they have no filters, and see what pops out of their mouths, or what they do. Maybe the heroine's best friend is sick of playing second fiddle and wants some attention and sets his desk on fire. Maybe the brutal mercenary spends all their time trying to feed the chickadees. Maybe the lady-in-waiting knew *all* the cuss words when she was six.

31. UNDERSCORE

My writer friend Marie Brennan spends time coming up with elaborate playlists for her books. Granted, not all writers can *write* to music, and some writers can only write to instrumental music or foreign songs because lyrics (that they can understand) distract them from the prose. But making a book playlist, with themes for specific characters, chapters, and locations, can be an excellent method of killing time if the story isn't moving anyway. This probably depends on how strongly you associate particular themes with their original contexts. I admit I got thrown out of one of her book "soundtracks" for a medieval-ish setting when I recognized a track from Jon Everist's score for *Battletech*, a video game involving stompy giant robots in the far future. But that's a pretty idiosyncratic response!

You can either literally put together a playlist the way Marie does, or you can write up notes as to what the score for your book would sound like, or (if you compose for a hobby, as I do) write the music yourself. Most of us who have grown up on film and TV are familiar with a lot of scoring clichés, whether that's a fanfare of six French horns when the cavalry arrives, creepy screeching noises and atonal pizzicato as people descend into the basement of a haunted house, or weepy, vibrato-y violins during an emotional reunion between two lovers.

Even if you don't produce a playlist, or produce the music (or hire someone else to do it for you), it can be useful to explicitly lay out notes to your book's "score" because it forces you to consider the *tone* and *emotion* of scenes over time, and how they contribute to the ebb and flow of *tension* and *resolution*. In fact, this emphasis on the interplay between tension/resolution was something I learned not from a book on writing craft, but from Jon Gindick's excellent *Country and Blues Harmonica for the Musically Hopeless*. Having a way to chart the emotions that you're trying to evoke in each scene or chapter can be a useful diagnostic tool when the story isn't landing the way you want it to. If you have a scene that strikes you as weepy violins and you really wanted it to be a French horn fanfare, then revisions are probably in order.

32. YELP REVIEWS

I sometimes like looking up Google or Yelp reviews for random places in my home city, Baton Rouge. Sometimes the search results are pretty funny. For example, I once did a search for "Jewish deli" (because I was hoping for delicious Jewish food) and the top hit was a place best known for its shrimp and grits. So, I'm not Jewish, but I double-checked with a Jewish friend, who confirmed that shrimp and grits may be very Southern (and delicious!) but they are no way no how Jewish (or kosher, for that matter).

Consider the places that appear in your story. What kind of Yelp reviews would they get? Even the kinds of places that aren't normally reviewed?

A vampire-haunted mausoleum might get "Excellent ambience for Halloween" or "Hosts don't understand personal boundaries, I demanded a refund." A medieval chateau might get "Beautiful views, especially at sunrise over the mountains, but it's drafty and there's no toilet paper." A diner on the interstate might get "Only has two items on the menu, burgers and coke. A nightmare for anyone who's vegan. Good service, though."

The places in our stories don't just exist in isolation (unless they do). They often have reputations based on the way people interact with them. It can be a lot of fun hinting at those reputations and the way they vary depending on who's doing the talking.

33. PICTURE THIS

I went to graduate school for secondary teacher education (to be a math teacher, in my case) and one of the assignments we received involved writing an essay, or quasi-essay, about the proper use of authority. I wrote and illustrated a quasi-essay on different facets of authority in the form of a children's book about animals. One of my professors asked me if I'd considered getting it published. It was a very flattering comment, but I'm pretty sure you can't have text talking blithely about things like "delegation" and "authoritarianism" in a children's picture book...(If I'm wrong, please let me know!)

Nevertheless, a fake (or real?) picture book can be a great way to zoom out from your book if you're getting stuck on the big picture (pun intended). If you're getting lost in the trees, consider doing a mockup of your book and its plot as a sixteen-page picture book (or however many pages works for you). You don't need to illustrate it yourself, although that can be fun, since most of us can at least manage stick figures. You could use pictures off the internet (for private use only), or grab some old print catalogues and magazines and do some collage.

I'm always in danger of getting tangled up in the intricacies of some intrigue or double-triple-quadruple cross in my books. It often helps me to think of ways to zoom out, to cook the story down to its barest essence. That essence won't include a lot of nuance or detail—but sometimes that's the point.

34. INNER SITH

Some of you are Jedi or paladin types, and then some of us are really Sith—powered by rage and spite. I've often told my husband that I don't write for the greater good of the world. I write because I'm a stubborn cuss and I want to wallop my manuscript into submission. If you're like me and you're having a tough time with motivation, maybe it's helpful to remember that rage and spite can be generative. That 8th grade teacher told you your writing was no good and you'd never make it? Well, you'll show her!

Some people work best with time-based goals (e.g. "I will write for one hour today," or "I will write three 25-minute sprints this week") and that's totally valid. I prefer wordcounts because deadlines stress me out. Do whatever works best for you!

I like to take "thinking breaks" every 100 words sort of as a mini reward-to-self. A couple acquaintances helped me code an app, Hundred Words, which rewards me every 100 words I write by showing me a picture from a curated collection on my computer. The web app Written? Kitten! (http://writtenkitten.co/) does much the same thing, except in a feline flavor.

Beyond that, I channel my Inner Sith by keeping track of my progress either in a locked blog entry or in a paper notebook. My goal is usually 1,500 words/day on a given project, so my Inner Sith musings might look like this:

100 words down, 1,400 words to fucking go!
200 words down, 1,300 words to fucking go!

(Aside: I once made a typo while journaling this by omitting a word and came out with *400 words down, 1,100 words to fucking!*, which, uh, made my writing motivation reward structure look VASTLY different from reality. Although if you're my husband and you're reading this, feel free to make me an offer...)

You get the idea. You don't have to say "fucking" if it bothers you, but for me one of the great joys of adulthood after going to a Christian private school is getting to use swear words. Use whatever mantra keeps you going! It could be *10 minutes down, 50 minutes left, I AM THE QUEEN OF WRITING!* It's just between you and your manuscript, after all!

35. BAD MATH

Well, okay. I majored in math (no one's perfect), and this trick isn't technically bad math. It's just math.

I used to write 2,000 words/day, mainly because I got into a rhythm of 4,000-word chapters. This way I would write half a chapter per working day. But one thing I noticed was that, for me, the first 1,000 words were relatively easy (to the extent that anything to do with writing is easy, anyway), and then the last 1,000 words would frequently be kind of a slog.

So I decided to play a stupid trick with myself and split up my 2,000-word target into two 1,000-word targets. I'd write my first 1,000 words, and then I'd reset and write another 1,000 words. After all, 1,000 + 1,000 = 2,000, is really all that's going on here. I wasn't taking a break between the two sessions, although that would be a logical next step. Somehow, splitting the larger goal into two half-sized goals fooled my brain into thinking I had two smaller easy tasks to do instead of one big hard one.

This trick might not work for you, especially if your brain is smarter than mine. But if you're dealing with the same phenomenon —finding that the second half of your writing day is much more a slog than the first half—give it a try. And take breaks if that helps! If breaking your writing up into more than one session is what works for you and your schedule, go for it!

36. GRAFFITI

I was once working on a personal art project that involved urban landscapes, back when we lived in Southern California. One of the things that fascinated me was the colorful and varied graffiti I saw in some parts of town, especially in Los Angeles. A friend and I once spotted a mysterious graffito dedicated to Epyon, a giant robot from the anime *Gundam Wing*. Before then it had never occurred to me that graffiti artists might be anime fans!

Anyway, I begged my husband to take me for a drive into Los Angeles so I could get some up-close-and-personal photography of choice graffiti. My husband, who has more common sense than I do, declined because he didn't want to be caught in "the bad part of town." The project died shortly afterward, although for reasons unrelated to the lack of graffiti pics.

Think about the locations in your story. What, if any, graffiti would they attract? The NSFW comic *Terminal Lance* makes numerous jokes about how penis graffiti shows up everywhere the US Marines do. I can't be the only one who grew up with school bathrooms featuring crudely penciled lovers' hearts and insults.

This can still be a useful thought experiment even if the location in question is too classy to *have* graffiti. Imagine a graffiti artist visiting your duke's castle, or your moose shifter's gym, or your star princess's dining room. What would they notice, and where would they add their "embellishments"?

37. TOURIST GUIDES FOR DRAGONS

Once upon a time, when I was a middle schooler in Texas, I was subjected to a class of Texas History. Texas's history is colorful, to say the least, and I was lucky enough to have an excellent teacher, Ms. Hampton, who taught the Gifted & Talented version of the course alongside GT English.

One of the things we learned as a matter of course was a basic version of Texas geography, specifically its major cities. This is the only reason that I know that Port Arthur, Beaumont, and Orange, three cities I have never visited, are called the Golden Triangle. Googling reveals the reason for the moniker is historical oil wealth. Thank you, internet!

Because this was the GT English-Texas History block, our assignments and exams often had a creative writing component to them. Our test on Texas geography was to be written in the form of a travel guide. Off-the-wall approaches were not only permitted but encouraged.

So when I wrote my exam, I did it in the form of a Tourist Guide to Texas—for traveling dragons. Because everything's better with dragons, right? I had fun coming up with draconic opinions on topics from horse racing to barbecue. Call me a Texas BBQ snob (I was born in Houston) but I think even a dragon would appreciate our ribs!

Maybe your setting, too, could use a Tourist Guide for Dragons! Or if dragons aren't your thing, you could substitute vampires, lamias, aliens...whatever works for you.

38. GESTALT D&D

This weird trick comes from two disparate places: a Dungeons & Dragons variant called Gestalt D&D and Gwen Hayes's book on writing structure/beats for category romance, *Romancing the Beat*.

The essence of Gestalt D&D is that you create character classes (e.g. fighter, cleric, mage, whatever) by *smashing together* two regular character classes and taking all the best bits to create a lean, mean, Frankenstein's monster machine. It doesn't notably produce *game balance*, but if you're playing with this variant that's not really the point. The *point* is to produce delightfully overpowered characters with combinations of abilities you normally wouldn't get to play.

Where does *Romancing the Beat* come in? One piece of advice that Hayes gives in that book and that has always stuck with me, even in non-romance contexts, is that a romance is the story of how they "go from hole-hearted to whole-hearted via love conquering all." Character A's hole is filled by something that Character B provides, and vice versa.

When I'm writing a team-up, whether of two or more characters, one of the things I want to know is how their strengths and weaknesses complement each other. How they *complete* each other, both emotionally and in terms of abilities. Sometimes I do this deliberately as I construct characters so that one is yin to the other's yang. Sometimes I start with the characters and have to figure out how they can support each other after the fact.

Smooshing the two (or more) characters together into a super-character who has access to the best traits of both can be one way of diagnosing when a team-up is or isn't working. Maybe you have two people who serve as muscle, and there's no one who can be a lookout or drive the getaway car or crack the safe. Getting your characters to make those contacts, or improvise a solution, can be an interesting plot point! Conversely, maybe your characters are *too* effective together at a time when you're trying to generate tension by making things tough for them, and you either need to upgrade your villain or find a way to knock out some of your heroes' capabilities.

39. ANNOTATIONS

When I was in high school, I haunted the nonfiction shelves because I loved learning about all the weird things in the wide world. One of the books I read was John Boswell's *Christianity, Social Tolerance, and Homosexuality*. I am not a scholar (I certainly wasn't as a teenager, anyway) but one of the things that fascinated me about that book was its footnotes! Sometimes there were so many footnotes that they took up half the page. Some of the footnotes were entirely in Greek or other languages that I couldn't read then and still can't now. But some of the footnotes were in English, and they weren't just citations, but offered opinionated and fascinating commentary.

Recently when I stopped by a bookstore, I saw that Neil Gaiman's *American Gods*, which I read some twenty years ago in college, now has a special annotated edition. I didn't buy it, but I got to thinking that annotating one of my own stories could be fun, if only there were more space in the margins.

Where this becomes generative is if you're reviewing your manuscript and need to come up with ideas springing from the text. If you're oppositional and motivated by spite, you might write fake notes by a scholar who takes everything out of context and misreads your work of genius. If you prefer cheerleading, you could write imagined words of praise or a learned exegesis.

You could even consider your story as a faux historical document, and consider what scholars or cranks would say in their footnotes. Heck, author/editor C. C. Finlay has a story that's told *entirely* in footnotes, originally published in *The Magazine of Fantasy and Science Fiction*, August 2001. It could be a great way to consider alternate perspectives and possibilities. How would a member of the Thieves' Guild annotate your hero's story? What would the local barista think of the romance between your two giraffe shifters?

40. REINCARNATION

I don't belong to a religious tradition that particularly believes in reincarnation, but take this in a spirit of fiction. At a workshop I once attended (Viable Paradise VIII), editor Teresa Nielsen Hayden described history as "the secret technology" of worldbuilding, no matter what genre you're writing in. Especially for genres like science fiction, fantasy, and sometimes horror, it's not always possible to research something exactly in a world that doesn't exist. But by looking at historical examples, you can often find something *close*.

The same can also be helpful when you're templating characters. If your character were a reincarnation of some historical figure, which one would it be and why? Or maybe your character *is* a fictional analogue of said figure, as in Kate Elliott's *Unconquerable Sun*, which posits a gender-swapped Alexander the Great in a space opera future, or Xiran Jay Zhao's *Iron Widow*, whose science-fictional heroine is loosely based on the historical figure Wu Zetian. No reason why you couldn't mash a few together, too, if you wanted.

You can also project a character into the future of your world—if they were reincarnated, how would they come back and why? What traits would they share and which ones would be different? Even if reincarnation doesn't literally exist in your setting, this sort of projection into the past and/or future is a nifty way of reimagining your character's essential traits.

41. RESURRECTION

If one of your characters could resurrect any figure from the past (theirs or someone else's), who would it be and why?

You don't have to do this literally! But I, personally, am frequently guilty of creating characters who float in a void with no past. This is okay when it's a minor one-line character, like the waiter who walks on to serve the cucumber sandwiches and then never shows up again in the story; in those cases, it's frequently *distracting* to the reader to have too much detail because the reader may wonder if this is an important, load-bearing part of the story when it actually isn't.

But oftentimes, if you do have an important, load-bearing character, they probably should have some sort of past history. I personally have never been able to go through one of those writer's checklists that you can find on the internet where you fill out the date of birth, astrological sign, place of birth, and so on down the line. (If those work for you, obviously, keep on keeping on!) So I have to approach the question sideways.

Not every character has a tragically dead figure in their past, of course. But a variant of this that's more generally applicable is, What figure from the past would your character like to sit down and have dinner with? Maybe your hard-nosed politician doesn't think anyone from the past has anything to offer her, and shrugs off the question. Maybe your gambler has someone they fleeced once, feels guilty about, and would like to apologize to. Maybe your reporter is dying to know what *really* happened at the Battle of the Three-Headed Stag!

42. "A DOZEN, A GROSS, AND A SCORE"

Some of us are good at the big picture, and some of us are good at fine details, and I'm sure there are also people who are good at both, lucky them. I am one of the former, and when I get stuck in a book, it's usually because I'm trying to concentrate too hard on fine details and getting myself knotted up. If you're a detail person, of course, this won't apply to you—getting granular will be generative for you rather than an obstacle course.

In any case, once upon a time, I was active in Legend of the Five Rings (L5R) fandom. L5R, as a collectible card game (think Magic: The Gathering, but themed around fantasy samurai), frequently released expansion packs, and those packs included cards that featured various characters or locations or events. People in the fandom would provide thoughtful commentary on the cards' effectiveness in the current tournament environment, create deck lists, and so on.

There was a brief period, on the other hand, where *my* claim to fame was creating L5R *limericks* based on every new card. The limericks sometimes commented on the card art, sometimes on the card mechanics, sometimes on the flavor text. Each one was a separate challenge. What can I say, I was in college and it wasn't the most destructive hobby I could have chosen.

You can fit a surprising amount of "plot" into a limerick, but you have to be efficient about it. And of course the constraint of the form —its meter and the rhyme scheme—forces you to get creative. It can take you to places that you wouldn't ordinarily think of.

If you're stuck on the big picture of a character or a story or a plot point, try summarizing it in limerick form and see if that shakes anything free.

> A collection of weird writing tricks
> Was written this year just for kicks.
> Just pick one and try it,
> Or shout it or sigh it,
> And maybe your book will be fixed.

(You thought this was going to be NSFW given the rhymes, didn't you.)

(I didn't say it had to be a *good* limerick!)

43. THE FAKE BROTHER

There's an anime I watched years ago (I won't name it in case anyone cares about spoilers) in which, at one point, the main character shows up after a brief time skip and lo! Suddenly he has a younger brother. The "brother" isn't *really* his brother and there are shenanigans afoot, but that vexed relationship provided some powerful moments in the story.

This particular anime had a well-connected cast of characters, but sometimes I find myself writing a story where the main character is *dis*connected. This can be a problem when I'm trying to motivate them, or when I want them to interact with some form of community in the world of the story.

I recently watched *The Expanse* (based on the books by James S. A. Corey), which features one great character (among many great characters!) that my friend, the writer Rachel Brown, described as a "serially monogamous one-person dog." This character always had a strong connection to someone in the season's cast. What made this particularly fascinating was that this character was also the crew's token sociopath! And yet that sense of *strong connection* made his scenes especially compelling.

You don't literally have to give a disconnected character a fake brother (or sister, or sibling, or whatever). But sometimes it's worth thinking about how connected they are, and, if warranted, how to *get* them connected to another character (or pet, or green onion plant, or whatever).

44. EMPIRE

There's a k-pop song by Wengie and Minnie (the latter from (G)I-DLE) called "Empire." When I looked up the lyrics, they were all about I HAVE ALL THE MONEY I AM FABULOUSLY RICH I AM THE QUEEN OF EVERYTHING, paired with stupendous visuals of the two singers as a pair of empresses. (I think. Interpreting K-pop videos can be a tricky business!) There's also a fascinating novella by K. J. Parker called "The Sun and I," which describes the crackalicious ascension of an "invented" religion, and I sometimes think of these two things in tandem.

If your character founded an empire based on their most core, cherished beliefs and desires, what would it look like? It doesn't have to be pretty. For that matter, you can run this thought experiment with antagonists and villains as well as heroes.

It doesn't have to be a literal empire, either. But surely we've all had moments of "If I ruled the world, there would always be freshly brewed French press coffee ready for me at 6 a.m." or "library books wouldn't have overdue fines." Even maybe "there would be telepathic machines to write our books for us." (I wish!)

Once that empire exists, or has at least been conceived, you can then start knocking holes into it. Is that French press coffee magically brewed, or is there an underclass of underpaid baristas who have to do the work rain or shine? Are there secret library book thieves who pretend that their books are perennially "overdue" and who sell them to paper magicians to be cut up for ritual purposes? Do the telepathic machines report on all your thoughts to the robot overlords?

If your character really ran that empire, how far would they go to maintain it, and what would they do in defense of those beliefs? Sure, they (probably?) won't get a *literal* empire, unless they're that one character from Brandon Sanderson's Mistborn series who does found an empire based on his ideals and lives to regret it. But you can explore those questions in the context of whatever your actual story is.

45. ORACLE

No, I'm not talking about the Oracle at Delphi! Rather, I mean what's known as "oracles" in solo roleplaying games and similar contexts, where you use a random number generator and a table (the "oracle") to generate a prompt that tells you what happens next, or what monster you're fighting, or what solemn vow your character has broken. A non-gaming version of this idea that you might have heard of if you're American is the Magic 8-Ball.

Obviously, the kind of story you get out of the oracle depends on the oracle itself. Ones for fantasy are probably the most common, if you want to use one that someone else made for inspiration. Inflatable Studios has a free "generic" oracle called One Page Solo Engine, for which a web app version is available.

But you might get more mileage out of custom-designing your own oracle if you can't find something specific to your genre or characters. For example, if I'm writing a science fiction thriller featuring psychic powers (I'm watching *Agents of S.H.I.E.L.D.* for the first time so I have this on the brain right now), I might have an oracle running on six-sided dice (d6's) with items like the following.

Character (roll 1d6)

1 = person with psychic powers
2 = secret agent
3 = hacker
4 = mad scientist
5 = corrupt CEO
6 = "femme fatale" of any gender

Setting (roll 1d6)

1 = coffee shop
2 = a sleepy farm town
3 = an abandoned warehouse
4 = the red-light district
5 = a museum
6 = secret HQ

Complication

1 = two agents quarrel
2 = an agent is kidnapped
3 = mutant super soldiers
4 = someone is a traitor
5 = a secret is exposed
6 = HQ has gone silent

By rolling a d6 three times, you generate a character, setting, and complication as the seeds for a scene. And you can customize tables to your liking—different dice, or a playing card draw, different answers to the rolls, different topics for the tables.

Even if you don't *use* the oracle, thinking about what *kinds* of things belong on these tables can itself help you figure out the structure and tropes of your story.

46. LACUNAE

This trick for unsticking yourself is simple, but for love of spork, either make a backup of your writing file or save a copy (Save As) first!

If you're stuck and can't figure out where to go next, go through a nice chunk of your manuscript, say the last five pages or so. Delete the first four words. Save the fifth. Delete the next four words (#5-9). Save the tenth. And so on.

(You see why I told you to make a backup or a copy?)

What you have left are a bunch of cryptic words. They're still *your* words, but they're no longer in the *sequence* or *context* that you had originally decided for them. Doing this with the first few paragraphs of my science fantasy book *Dragon Pearl* gets me this, for instance:

stranger's liked I it meant the my me do units house few sure enough aunties filters dust I life counting turned years take the and into all the though I threadbare sleep begun the

This is hash nonsense, which is the *point*. Now it's time to take as many of these words as you can and write something using them, or words related to them.

The stranger really liked me, even if the few houses in this part of the city were owned by my horrible aunties. The filters here kept out the dust. My life depended on it. I could count the years I had remaining by the thick, pungent silt that accumulated on them. Every morning I woke from a threadbare sleep, wondering how much longer before my real life would begin—before the stranger would take me off-planet as she had promised.

The point is not that this is deathless prose (this isn't much more than hash nonsense itself), but it gives you a starting point and forces you to write to a constraint. If part of your brain is balking, it's sometimes possible to sneak up on it with tricks like this one.

47. FRESHMAN ORIENTATION

I arrived a week early to college (Cornell University) for freshman orientation, like many students. The single thing I remember most vividly was a meeting that freshmen at my dorm had with a sorority girl. She gave us the usual disclaimers about waiting until we were actually legal to drink alcohol, and then some tips on drinking safely, like Never Accept An Opened Drink In Case It Has Roofies. I was sufficiently impressed by this warning that I made a point of never, ever setting foot in a fraternity or sorority, or attending a party, mainly because I want to live an excessively boring life. I'm sure other things happened during orientation but foxed if I can remember them.

Indeed, my general caution was to serve me well. Cornell, located in Ithaca, NY, is known for its rugged terrain (hence the pun "Ithaca is gorges"). Cascadilla Gorge separates part of the campus from Collegetown. My sophomore year, when I was a peer writing tutor, an unlucky freshman got drunk, went for a walk along Cascadilla Gorge, slipped, and fell to his death. I remember it because one of my tutees, also a freshman, had known him and was having difficulty concentrating on an essay he had due because of his shock and grief. I told him to explain the situation to his professor and ask for an extension, although I never found out if he actually got it. (I hope so.) I've climbed up the side of that gorge (I was *not* drunk, although it was still a damn fool thing to do) and I remember how it was littered with beer cans and broken bottles.

The world of your book is undoubtedly full of pitfalls of its own. Maybe they're dramatic and potentially deadly, like the gorge. Maybe they're more light-hearted—the deacon's wife is very particular about her tea, or the yarn shop's resident dragon insists on being bribed with an oatmeal cookie before it will let anyone near the qiviut yarn. What would a "freshman orientation guide" to your setting include?

48. SUPERPOWER

For over twenty years, I've been asking my husband (since before he *was* my husband, in fact) what his favorite superpower is. I've never been able to get a straight answer out of him if I disallow meta answers like "the power that lets you have all powers." (My husband is the kind of rules lawyer who should not be allowed near a genie.)

We have a household joke that I'm the person who got the absolutely terrible "superpower" of perfect pitch. There are some uses for perfect pitch, but for most purposes, relative pitch is just as good, and far less annoying. (I am incapable of listening to a cappella groups unless they're Carnegie Hall levels of good, for example, and first-year violin players are right out.) There's a roleplaying game system called HERO, mostly intended for superheroes, in which perfect pitch is a dinky five-point power, as opposed to something like laser eyebeams. An acquaintance who was former Navy once consoled me by telling me that I would have made an excellent sonar person, but that ship has sailed (pun intended).

What is the superpower that your character wishes they had? If they already have one, they might want something else. A shapeshifter might envy a teleporter. Or perhaps their idea of a "superpower" is something more mundane. The guy with laser eyebeams might wish for the ability to bake perfect bread every time. They might even want my *other* dinky "superpower," which is that I can sleep on airplanes. (The reason it sucks is that I have insomnia in my own bed! Kind of a bad trade-off.) "Super" is, after all, in the eye of the beholder.

49. THE KING AND THE BEGGAR

There are probably earlier antecedents for the "role swap" story than the fairytale of the king and the beggar who swap places. I'm not a folklorist, though, so I won't worry about tracking down the history.

If you want to generate additional tension, especially with two characters who are hypercompetent in their areas of expertise, one thing you can do is force them to swap roles. The duelist is unbeatable with a sword in hand, but socially inept. The diplomat can charm the hooves off a giraffe at a hundred paces, but sucks at fighting. Stick them in a situation where they have to do each other's jobs, perhaps because they're in the wrong place at the wrong time, and start twisting the screws.

You can have additional fun with this scenario by having characters *learn* each other's skills or roles, perhaps in the context of a special mission, or in order to fool or outwit someone. The TV show *Orphan Black*, which is centered around a group of clones with different specialties, used this conceit a lot, with clone A disguising herself as clone B in order to carry out a task that the enemy didn't realize she had the skills for.

You can also use this as a diagnostic tool if the character balance in your story doesn't seem quite right. In most instances, your characters *shouldn't* be interchangeable. If you put your duelist into the diplomat's council and the scene runs exactly the same as if the diplomat were still there, this is probably a sign that your characters aren't differentiated enough. You might need to make each one more individual, or merge two characters into a single one if the extra one is redundant.

50. RAINBOW TIME

Here's one for the more visually-oriented of you. I'm not a visual person, but even I find myself drawn to certain colors and color combinations, and repelled by others. And I can't be the only person who was influenced at an impressionable age by Carole Jackson's *Color Me Beautiful*, which divides people of different colorations into four "seasons" and prescribes the colors that she says will make you look best. Fashion isn't my area of expertise (I go around in a T-shirt and leggings most days, and 90% of my outerwear is either black or gray) but I often think of that book when I'm clothing my *characters*.

If you have a collection of markers or coloring pencils or gel pens, you can have fun creating color palettes that reflect your major characters' personalities. If you're writing the kind of book that has factions or color-coding like Anne McCaffrey's Dragonriders of Pern or George R. R. Martin's Houses in A Song of Ice and Fire/*Game of Thrones*, you probably want the factions/Houses/etc. to have colors (or symbols) that reflect *their* vibe. Your faction of stone-cold, brutal mercenaries and assassins is probably going to have a hard time being taken seriously if their house colors are blush pink and mint. (Unless you're trying to *subvert* the stereotype, in which case, have at it!) And making sure that a variety of colors are represented will help ensure that your characters aren't all depressive Goth types. (I may be guilty of this.)

If the issue is the ups and downs of your plot, try making color palettes for each of your scenes or chapters (whichever unit of story makes more sense for you). Maybe that chapter where your characters are all trapped in a dungeon overrun by slime molds evokes black and rust and dingy greens for you, while the dinner party with the duchess puts you in mind of sparkling silver and gold and a splash of vibrant royal blue. By charting these color palettes against the passage of chapters, you can get a visual representation of the moods/settings of your plot. Maybe you discover that your book spends too long in "dungeon colors" and you'd really rather have it be more light-hearted.

For a bonus, you might enjoy Patti Bellantoni's book on color in cinematography, *If It's Purple Someone's Gonna Die*, but the important thing is that you use a color schema that makes sense to you.

51. FRANCE HAS A ROSE

Here's a worldbuilding trick for those of you who write in secondary worlds, or otherwise have made-up nations or political units.

There's a webcomic/manga/anime by the slightly alarming title of *Axis Powers Hetalia* by Hidekaz Himaruya, slightly notorious in the anime/manga fan community in my glancing encounters with it. You don't need to read it! In fact, I haven't read it. (I was too chicken.) All you need to know is the premise, which is WWI and WWII told with anthropomorphic nations. That's right: France, Japan, Italy, etc. are all represented as human characters.

One thing I sometimes get hung up on is differentiating my made-up fictional nations without drawing too closely from history (although there's nothing wrong with actualfax historical fiction) or making them too cartoonishly different. It can be helpful thinking of each nation as an archetypal person—the kind of person who would appear in something in *Hetalia*, or else in one of those old-timey single-panel political cartoons where Uncle Sam with his top hat stands in for the USA and so on.

There's also no need to restrict your nation to a single archetypal person, if you're the kind of writer who enjoys coming up with nuances early in the process. (As I've said before, I need archetypes almost to the point of caricature because of the way my brain works, but everyone's process is different.) You could come up with several different characters to represent different national "types."

Worldbuilding-wise, national archetypes *and* stereotypes are something that really show up in life, and that might appear in your fictional cultures! When I was in middle school, I wanted to take German for my foreign language because one of my best friends was half-German. My parents made me take French instead because French was more "cultural," as though Beethoven, Goethe, and Rainer Maria Rilke counted for nothing! (I suspect Mom was biased because her older sister, my oldest aunt, got a Ph.D. in French literature. These days, I'm doing Duolingo German, so I guess I won in the end?)

Sometimes these archetypes/stereotypes can be surprising! I remember finally reading an abridged translation of Vegetius' *De Re Militari* (*On Military Matters*). Vegetius, a Roman, spoke disparagingly of the small stature and uninspiring physiques of Roman men, as opposed to the big, vigorous German barbarians. This is definitely different from the super-macho image of Roman legionaries I'd gotten from movies—the divergence between expectation and reality can be something else you can play with.

52. ARTILLERY STRIKE OR BUST!

One of the things I did to research writing military science fiction was, believe it or not, looking up military *jokes*. This included an extremely enlightening romp through former Marine and artist Maximilian Uriarte's webcomic *Terminal Lance*, which has also spawned several print versions. At the time I read it, it was frequently NSFW—Marine humor is not for the delicate soul—so proceed with caution!

There was also a really entertaining joke that I am failing to Google the source for that was about how to identify your enemy by what they do after you shoot at them. It went something like: If they respond with machine gun fire, they're Germans. If they respond with disciplined rifle fire, they're British. And if nothing happens for fifteen minutes, but you're then suddenly wiped out by an artillery strike, they're Americans.

Another funny one concerned the different Armed Forces branches, and was told to me by a military buff friend, David Gillon. It went something like this: If you tell the Army to secure a building, they'll surround it with armor and heavy infantry, and not let anyone out until they receive orders to. If you tell the Marines the same thing, they'll storm the building, eliminate any resistance, and not let anyone enter until they receive orders to. If you tell the Navy that, they'll turn out the lights, close and lock all doors and windows, and post a watch. If you tell the Air Force that, they'll take out a 30-year lease with an option to buy.

You may not be writing military science fiction, as I sometimes do. But chances are there are either institutions or groups or individuals in your story who can be characterized not only by the kinds of jokes they tell (if they have a sense of humor), but the kinds of jokes told *about* them. Personally, when I had to come up with fake soldier jokes about a military faction, the Kel, known for suicidal bravery, I resorted to adapting viola jokes: *What's the difference between a violin and a Kel? The Kel burns longer.* (I used to play viola, so I'm entitled!)

53. HIT BY A BUS

I made a habit in college of taking almost every class in the history department that had the word "war" in it, mainly for writing research purposes. One of those classes was Prof. Barry S. Strauss's War and Diplomacy on the Korean Peninsula, which was of particular interest to me as a Korean-American. The two wars covered by that class were the Imjin War (1592-1598), in which Japan, under the leadership of Hideyoshi, invaded Korea (with eventual designs on China and India) and was repelled by Korea's Admiral Yi Sun-Shin, plus the Korean War, which is not resolved as of this writing despite starting in 1950. (The "hot" part of the war "ended" with an ongoing armistice.)

One of the concepts covered in our discussion of the Imjin War was that of the "bench strength" of an army. Pretty much every Korean knows that Admiral Yi Sun-Shin was the architect of Korea's successful defense at sea. (If you've never heard of this before, please don't worry—it's local history and people outside East Asia frequently aren't familiar with it.) Admiral Yi went undefeated, despite being too loyal for his own good and also being so bad at politics that, despite his victories, he was at one point jailed by his own king and tortured. (I wish I was making this up.)

It seems pretty clear that Admiral Yi's leadership of the Korean navy was instrumental in the victories at sea, because the one battle that was commanded by a rival, Admiral Won Kyun, ended in a disastrous defeat for the Koreans. Same navy, different admiral. Due to the rout, Admiral Yi was reinstated, and pulled off a victory at the Battle of Myeongnyang despite now being outnumbered ten to one. The key variable is the leadership.

There are probably other historical examples showing how leadership affects the effectiveness of an army (President Abraham Lincoln's struggle to find an effective general in the American Civil War comes to mind?) but this is the one that I happen to be the most familiar with.

Anyway, bench strength. Our class had a great discussion one afternoon as to whether Korea would have survived the invasion if someone had successfully assassinated Admiral Yi. It seemed pretty clear that Korea got really lucky and that there was likely no other general/admiral of his caliber available to step up if something happened to him. (I say "general/admiral" because the Korean armed forces were a unified service, and the Korean words for those two ranks are the same even though they're different in English. Yi started out in an infantry posting before he was promoted to "admiral.")

If you look at your band of heroes, or your band of villains, what is their bench strength? Is there a leader without whom they would fall apart? If someone were hit by a bus, would they be able to carry on—is there a contingency plan? If you were to assassinate a single person to destroy your heroes' chances, who would that person be? Even if the heroes do have a backup or a contingency, is that key person the hero themselves? And if not, why? There isn't a wrong or right answer to this. It's just something to take under consideration.

54. RESCUE CATS

Like many writers, I am owned by a catten, who is a rescue named Cloud. She is a very lovely dilute tortoiseshell, and she likes to "help" me write by sitting in front of my keyboard and blocking my view of the monitor with her fur face. I'm sure this is a familiar phenomenon to any cat owner.

My friend Ursula and I occasionally text each other pictures of our cats. She has two; I only have the one, with good reason. Cloud, who is so amiable and friendly to *humans*, turns into a ferocious heat-seeking missile when loosed in the company of *other cats*. We discovered this after Hurricane Ida when our power was knocked out and we sheltered for a week with some friends in Texas, Stephanie and Toby. They own two cats, and my daughter, in a spirit of optimism and experimentation, let Cloud out of the guest room. Cloud *immediately* tracked and chased after the poor host cats, growling like a demon.

The now-defunct (or perhaps renamed) cat shelter from which we'd adopted Cloud had told us some things about her that proved to be accurate, and some less so. They told us, for instance, that she was not playful: true. Cloud is friendly but not very bright. 90% of cat toys meet with a confused expression and a refusal to move. They also told us that she had to be an Only Cat, because she did not get along with other cats: *very* true. And then they told us that she was a lap cat: eh. She's happy to be picked up and carried (she is the world's limpest cat), and she likes to sleep on me, and she likes to snuggle, but in terms of *literally* sitting in a lap, I've never been able to get her to do that.

Ursula once linked me to a hilarious compilation of descriptions of cats awaiting adoption, but the specific theme of the compilation was "describing cats who are clearly assholes by trying to make them sound like they're *not* assholes." I seem to have lost track of the link (for all I know, there's more than one such compilation) but here's a typical example from my own local cat shelter, paraphrased (and with the identity changed to protect the guilty):

Jinx is a loving cat who is purrfect for anyone seeking a constant companion. She will follow you everywhere you go and demand to be picked up and cuddled! In fact, once you pick her up, she will cling to you with her cute ickle claws and refuse to be put back down! Come by the adoption center today to meet Jinx and give her a furever home!

I remember reading "Jinx"'s description and thinking, Oh hell no I am not signing up for this cat experience. I like a cuddly cat, but I don't want one who demands to be picked up at every opportunity *and refuses to be put back down!*

So imagine that your characters, present or potential, are in a character shelter and that you are the shelter volunteer who has to write a description that will entice an author to "adopt" them into a story. What would that description look like? Especially if your character has some asshole tendencies?

(If your characters are all lovable cinnamon rolls, I apologize! I'm sure your characters are much more adoptable than my own murderous asshole soldier characters.)

On the other hand, if you're having one of those terrible, horrible, no-good, very bad writing days (most of us endure them once in a while, I daresay), a fun way to let off steam is to write a "please adopt me" description for your *book*. You know, something like this:

> *The Great American Novel is a thrilling literary experience in need of an experienced and expert author to take it firmly in hand. Ready for the challenge of wrangling a cast of hundreds, trimming down dozens of entangled storylines and cutting out unneeded tangents, and putting the events in chronological order? YOU are the one who can find undying fame and fortune by writing this book!*

55. PHILATELY

When I was younger, I had a number of pen pals. This was a side-effect of growing up largely before the internet was a thing, and of moving every few years. The only way to keep in touch with people without spending a fortune on (sometimes international) phone bills was to write letters. I had pen pals in Germany, Poland, and the USA, and of course I had family in South Korea.

As another side-effect, I accumulated a collection of stamps! I was fascinated by how the *aesthetic* of different countries was expressed in their stamps, and I dabbled in philately as a hobby. I used to have a ton of Korean stamps that featured every native flower and bird imaginable, from the mugunghwa (South Korea's national flower, also known in the West as the rose of Sharon) to hoopoe birds.

After my grandfather passed away, my sister and I even got our hands on some older stamps from my dad's childhood collection, miraculously preserved. The Czechoslovakian stamps included engraved drawings of clipper ships, while there were savanna animal stamps in the shapes of trapezoids from Tanzania.

I also enjoyed learning oddments of history from those stamps, although thirty years later I don't remember any details beyond a stamp that immortalized the American Revolution's "one if by land, two if by sea. My favorites—and I wish I remembered them more clearly—were a couple stamps that had a couple sentences of background history on the *back*, in small blue letters, like a secret.

Depending on the genre and time period you're writing, you may or may not be dealing with literal postage stamps. But how would you tell your story as a series of postage stamps or their equivalents? Which heroes and historical figures would be lionized with stamps of their own? Which flowers and cities and sporting events would be honored? What would be the approved official art styles and artists?

56. CHAPTER HEADERS

Every so often, I come across a book that has chapter headers that give a (usually partial) summary of what's to come, like the teaser of a TV episode. (Okay, I guess this is backwards; I'm sure this convention predates TV.) For example, the first few chapters of an epic fantasy might have headers that go like this:

Wherein Our Hero discovers that he is not truly a lowly scullery boy after all, but that the blood of the dragon kings runs in his veins and that all this time he could have been learning swordplay and heraldry instead of the nuances of effluvia and soap.

Wherein a surprise attack on the village forces Our Hero to evacuate with a mysterious hooded stranger and Our Hero's favorite chicken, Henny.

Wherein the mysterious stranger reveals herself as the last assassin-mage sworn to the line of the dragon kings, and Our Hero is forced to make a difficult decision regarding Henny.

You get the idea.

Not every book wants to have actual chapter headers in the *final draft*, but if you're stuck in the middle, or else having trouble with revisions, why not give them a go? Remember, the point of headers like this is to act like the "preview" for a TV episode. Bonus points if you make them as deliberately misleading as possible. Maybe Our Hero has the blood of the dragon kings in his veins not because he's a lost heir but because this is an unusual fantasy land with *very advanced medical technology* and through some mix-up he got a blood transfusion from a royal personage in his sickly youth.

57. APPS

You ever notice how there's an app for damn near everything these days, if you're a person who uses smartphones or tablets? As a gamer, I sometimes need to be able to just draw a card from a shuffled poker deck (for a solo RPG, say), and I found an app for that on iOS. My iPhone is a hot mess, including apps for Tarot, mate-in-one chess puzzles, various actual modern games (the one I play the most is a deckbuilder called Star Realms from Wise Wizard Games), a dice rolling app...okay, you've detected my bias as a random gamer. But I also have apps for high intensity workouts (sadly neglected in favor of walking, fencing, and exercise biking), speech synthesis (which can't handle weirdo sci-fi names, it turns out), and ear training (musical intervals). Apps everywhere!

If your story were an app, or spawned an app, what kind of app would it be? Since this is an imaginary app, the sky's the limit. Don't feel constrained by technological limitations or a budget for the art or the operating system (unless those constraints help your creativity, of course)! What app concept captures the *essence* of your book?

Maybe a rom-com would be a dating app that magically weeds out all the jerks. (If only!) Your stirring space opera might be one of those gripping real-time-strategy games with big explosions. I suspect a real war would end up getting represented much more realistically by the humble spreadsheet. A cozy mystery that involves chasing clues through the library system might be a book cataloging app with some Easter eggs built in, or that has certain special book titles/authors in cipher!

58. "BUT SOFT, WHAT LIGHT THROUGH YONDER WINDOW BREAKS?"

I apologize in advance to any poets, English teachers, and literature professors in the audience, but due to the vagaries of my high school education, I never properly learned the differences between most of the poetic feet (dactyls and trochees and so on). We had some English teachers at my high school who felt this was worth teaching and who therefore taught it in 9th or 10th grade. I had the teachers who didn't bother with the topic, and I never worked up the energy to look up and memorize the feet on my own initiative.

I *did* learn iambs, mainly because we read Shakespeare in English class and it was impossible to escape iambic pentameter. I was skeptical at first, partly because of the hype, partly because I'm not into romances and they always start you off with *Romeo and Juliet*. I didn't realize that, despite the titular lovebirds, *Romeo and Juliet* is a *tragedy*. (Imagine trying to fob off "hero dies of poison due to despair and heroine kills herself with a sword upon finding her lover dead" as a Happily Ever After on today's romance readers! It would be one-star reviews as far as the eye could see. Uh, hope it's okay to spoil a four-century-old play...) If someone had sold the play to me based on its *dead people* factor, bloodthirsty ninth-grade me would have been much more enthusiastic about it. But I digress.

As a refresher, iambic pentameter consists of lines made of five iambs (each one going "soft-LOUD"). So a line would go like this:

soft-LOUD soft-LOUD soft-LOUD soft-LOUD soft-LOUD

Or, to quote the Bard himself:

but SOFT what LIGHT through YON-der WIN-dow BREAKS

You can guess where this is going, right? If you're stuck on dialogue—it's all coming out flat or uninspired or on the nose—try upping the difficulty level by writing it in iambic pentameter! If you're feeling really brave, make it rhyme as well. (Dealer's choice on the rhyme scheme.)

> *"This battle dooms us all," the captain said.*
> *"From dusk to dawn the bombing hurts us all.*
> *No soldier soundly sleeps within their bed,*
> *And following these orders, we will fall."*

It doesn't have to be *good* verse! My example certainly isn't. The point is just to get unstuck by coming at the problem slantwise.

59. REDACTED

While writing a science fiction novel in which I made a passing mention of redacted text, I learned from one of my beta readers, a security architect, that even redaction has its pitfalls. There are ways to recover text from a redaction and you have to redact in certain ways to prevent that from happening. If you even skim security engineering papers, you find out all sorts of amazing things, like the fact that people can sometimes recover passwords based on the smudges on a phone's touchscreen. It's a scary world out there! (If this sort of thing is of interest to you, I recommend Ross Anderson's *Security Engineering*, whose second edition is available for free online. If you don't mind skimming the technical bits on, say, computer chip manufacturing and architecture, it's surprisingly accessible.)

I have security levels and classification on the brain because I've been watching *Agents of S.H.I.E.L.D.* lately, and they've mentioned everything from Level 1 to Level 10 (that I know of). If you were classifying parts of your book from your own characters, which parts would you keep from them so they didn't derail the plot in an attempt to escape their fates? Which would be the critical Level 10 secrets, as opposed to the Level 1 clues that are easily figured out?

Of course, this works better with some genres than others. Typical romance characters, assured of a Happily Ever After or Happy For Now ending, might just want to suck it up and take what comes! "Redshirts" in an espionage thriller or a military action-adventure or a horror novel might, of course, feel differently.

60. LESSON PLAN

The first time I saw a lesson plan for one of my books, it was the weirdest experience. I was torn between feeling flattered that someone thought this would be useful to teachers teaching my book *Dragon Pearl* (it's a middle grade space opera) and wondering if this meant that my book would traumatize a generation of youngsters who would then grow up hating everything I wrote.

I mean...writers are usually people who love books, so I was that kid who had to read Mildred D. Taylor's *Roll of Thunder, Hear My Cry* for 4th grade English and was so entranced that I went out and read everything else by Taylor that I could find in the library. On the other hand, that was 4th grade. By the time I reached high school, I was a more jaded and resentful reader, so when I was forced to read Thomas Hardy's *Tess of the d'Urbervilles* for 12th grade, I despised it so much that I not only swore that I would never read any other Hardy novel, but that I would never take another literature class, a promise I have kept.

Nevertheless, it's sometimes useful (and humbling) to look at your book through the eyes of a teacher. What would lesson plans for your book look like? What literary techniques would turn up? What context and vocabulary would the students need to learn to appreciate your book properly? What activities and assignments would they do, and what rubrics would they be graded on?

Full disclosure: I am not an English/literature teacher, so I don't know what real-world best practices are here. I have a M.A. in secondary *math* education, but one of the things they hammered into us over and over at Stanford is that teaching methods are particular to the *subject being taught*. And math pedagogy is, as far as I can tell, pretty different from English/literature pedagogy!

61. GRAPHOLOGY

One of my hobbies during childhood was graphology, the pseudoscience of "divining" people's personality traits from their handwriting. As I understand it, there is zero reliable scientific basis for this, but I was that kid who believed in aliens, Kirlian auras, and ley lines because they were shelved in the nonfiction section of the library. (I should also note at this point that graphology should not be mistaken for its much more reputable cousin graphanalysis, which involves forensic examination of handwritten documents, or graphology in the linguistic sense.)

My interest in handwriting came about because of Santa Claus letters. When my sister and I were young, we believed in Santa Claus, like many kids. Santa Claus had a habit of leaving us Christmas notes along with the gifts.

But we inevitably grew older and more skeptical, so we decided to leave Santa Claus a test to *prove* he was Santa Claus. (Staying up all night didn't work because neither my sister nor I was capable of staying awake that long.) We wrote Santa a letter asking him to name all his reindeer.

This was maybe a mean trick. I need to explain at this point that my parents were born and raised in South Korea, and a lot of the popular culture around Christmas is very different when it exists at all. (For example, many Koreans like going out to a fancy dinner on Christmas, which would be trickier in the USA, where most restaurants are closed on that day.) Dad, a music-lover, may have raised us on carols like "Silver Bells" (his favorite) and "O Holy Night," but he was kind of vague on the fine points of American Christmas traditions.

In any case, the card that Santa left us when we checked the next morning went something like this:

I'm sorry, I'm too old and I have forgotten the names of the reindeer except Rudolph. Merry Christmas!
  Love, Santa

Dad knew at least the *title* of "Rudolph the Red-Nosed Reindeer" but had apparently forgotten the rest of the lyrics, and this was long before the days when you could simply Google information. Beyond the excuse, though, what clinched it that Santa Was Dad was that I paid close attention to handwriting as a habit, and I pointed out to my sister that "Santa"'s handwriting was an *exact* match for our dad's!

I continued paying attention to handwriting just as an art—I often find the differences in individuals' handwriting styles, whether cursive or block letters or calligraphy or comic lettering, very beautiful. Of course, I no longer believe that handwriting is a way to predict personality traits.

HOWEVER. A fun way to take a character inventory is to treat graphology as though it were real, and go through a graphology inventory (Googling "graphology test" will bring up some options if you don't want to shell out on a handbook), picking out the personality traits that apply to the character you're designing or who has walked into your story. Even more fun, if you have some time to kill, is to use a graphology inventory to *design your character's (Roman alphabet) handwriting.*

62. TSR MAIL ORDER HOBBY SHOP

If your story is *already* based on a roleplaying game or adventure, you can give this one a miss. Otherwise, read on!

My sister and I share a collection of tabletop roleplaying game (TTRPG) books, which, along with the rest of our book collection, we consider to be a single library split across two households due to the exigencies of geography.

The two of us grew up in something of a roleplaying desert. At the time we were living in South Korea, TTRPGs were not well-known. We managed to obtain the Dungeons & Dragons "red box" but were foxed as to how to play a game designed for four to six players plus a gamemaster (GM) when it was just the two of us. We ended up having one person GM and the other run a full party (ironically taking the experience back closer to its origins in Chainmail, which we didn't learn about until much later) to run the included adventure.

Dungeons & Dragons and, to some extent, the Fighting Fantasy gamebooks were our gateway drug into gaming. But it was, at the time, a difficult hobby to pursue from South Korea, especially if you wanted English-language materials. We somehow got our hands on an RPG mail-order catalogue from the TSR Mail Order Hobby Shop, our only hope.

We were convinced for years that the two of us singlehandedly killed the TSR Mail Order Hobby Shop! The reason is that we pored over that catalogue and narrowed down our selections (Earthdawn, Ars Magica, other games from that era) and begged, begged, begged our dad until he agreed that we could put down his credit card number and put in a mail order. We waited months after sending the order form to the United States, in an agony of anticipation. Were we ever going to get our order?

Our order did in fact arrive, with all the games we had ordered— and a sad, sad notice that the TSR Mail Order Hobby Shop was closing down. We'd killed it! Our source of RPGs was dead! In fact, we learned years later that TSR had been having financial problems for some time, and that the timing was a coincidence. We were probably lucky to receive our order at all, given the circumstances.

In any case, one thing my sister and I rapidly discovered was that (a) every damn RPG rulebook or scenario book had a section that *only* the GM was supposed to read, and (b) we sucked at resisting temptation. The RPG adventures that we obtained were generally designed for a GM plus four to six players, and there were only two of us. So why not spoil ourselves? Years later, I learned that players reading things they weren't supposed to was *really common* among gamers. (Or maybe my friends are an unusually scurrilous bunch.)

RPG scenarios, adventures, or campaigns run the gamut from those that offer just the slightest adventure hooks (like Legend of the Five Rings' "Challenge, Focus, Strike") and micro-adventures/settings (as in Tiny Frontiers), to more elaborate adventures that account for multiple possible player decisions or which detail entire locations (cities, nations) for the players' exploratory impulses. Some come with or require pregenerated characters, while others are open to any characters the players can dream up.

It can be an interesting exercise to ask yourself how you'd convert your story and its plot and world into an adventure for other characters to experience—what they might do differently, what the decision points would be, what the possible outcomes could be—and how you might present that to a willing GM!

63. A CARE PACKAGE

My husband and I have rather divergent tastes in fiction. He likes heroic characters, or occasionally the fallen hero who is working very hard on redemption. I like clever antiheroes: one of my favorite authors is K. J. Parker, whose fantasy novels frequently showcase objectively horrible people (or, occasionally, poor sods destroyed by objectively horrible people). He likes "mechanistic" magic systems that are treated with scientific rigor—this household buys Brandon Sanderson in hardcover on the day of release—whereas I prefer more metaphorical, less mechanistic magic like those that appear in Patricia A. McKillip's later fantasies, such as *A Song for the Basilisk* or *Alphabet of Thorns*.

Another area where our tastes diverge: hurt/comfort (h/c). He enjoys that dynamic in stories. I don't hate it as such—I've read h/c stories I've enjoyed—but I don't seek it out, either.

Some books lend themselves much more to the h/c dynamic than others. Anything with camaraderie or found family or romance can go in that direction. My own works rarely feature that character dynamic.

Still, even if your story doesn't *literally* feature h/c, chances are that your characters will face harm or injury. Or maybe you're writing cozy mystery or the kind of cottagecore fiction where nothing really bad happens to anyone, but someone might enjoy a care package.

If you were putting together a first aid or emergency kit for your characters, what would be in it? It might include more unusual items or even critters. Maybe that gruff security guard would secretly adore a chance to spend a couple hours with a therapy dog. Maybe the thief always packs earbuds because music is what keeps them from freaking out in a stressful situation (and doubles as a disguise element). Maybe the commando carries a roll of duct tape everywhere, just in case.

And for gentler genres, it could be a care package rather than something that anticipates bad times or injury. A tin of delicious Mexican hot chocolate, or a tiny tinted-paper sketchbook with glitter gel pens, or an ickle potted succulent. Everyone needs comfort in some form or another.

64. AGONY AUNT

My latest confession is that I used to hate-read advice columns. (Well...I still read Ask A Manager, but that's not *hate*-reading.) You know the kinds of letters that would come in: "My spouse/significant other/partner is handsome/beautiful, clever, smart, rich, wealthy, cooks delicious breakfasts, great in bed, perfect in every way EXCEPT..." And there would always be an EXCEPT (in capital letters) or they wouldn't be writing to a stranger for advice as to how to fix their marriage/relationship/whatever. I say "hate-read" because half the time I hated the person who was writing in for being un-self-aware-ly an asshole, half the time I hated whoever the letter-writer was complaining about for obviously being an asshole, and half the time (yes, I realize that's three-halves) I hated the columnist's asshole advice. It's a conundrum.

Still...unless you're writing complete fluff (and maybe even if you are), characters in novels tend to wind up in passels of trouble. If *your* character were driven to ask for advice (anonymously, of course), what letter would they send in? Perhaps the farmgirl heroine would complain about the bully who cheats at halberdier lessons. Perhaps the lovesick businessperson would ask how to find out if the object of their affections is also into knifeplay. Perhaps the conniving thief would want to know how to disable the guardian automata that prevent him from stealing from the Embellished Palace.

Maybe someone would write in *knowing* that their friends/enemies are going to read the letter, and use it to seed disinformation!

For bonus points, make your antagonist secretly the columnist/advice-giver, and go to town with their answer!

65. "SUSURRUS"

My friends don't mock me about The Days of Susurrus anymore, although they totally could and I would deserve it.

What were The Days of Susurrus, you ask? This goes back to my fantasy trunk novel, *Origami Souls* (or various other titles—it went through a half-dozen of them), which I wasted ten years of my life writing and rewriting. A couple versions of it featured a magically enforced peace. Basically if you attempted to do violent things, magical forces would gather with a "susurrus" murmuration sound effect and kill you before you could do the violent thing. (I did not have much of a sense of irony when I was younger.)

Irony aside, the unfortunate side-effect of this bit of ridiculous worldbuilding was that the word "susurrus," which is weird and draws attention to itself, appeared every other page. "Susurrus" rapidly lost all meaning, the way your name ceases to have meaning after you've signed a few hundred bookplates.

If you're asking why my beta readers didn't complain, *trust me*, they complained. They complained very nicely. I think some of them were thinking of staging an intervention. But I was young and hotheaded *and I loved that word*.

And remember, this was the trunk novel I worked on for *ten years*.

That's a *lot* of "susurrus." Dear Reader, I bet *your* eyes are already crossing every time you see that word!

Some of you are lucky and don't have a problem with some Overused Pet Word. But maybe some of you are like me. Figure out what your "susurrus" is, and replace it with (a) a regular word (or regular *words*, if you're lucky to have multiple options) (b) that means the opposite. What does that do to your story?

Also, for love of God don't replace *your* Overused Pet Word with "susurrus," unless *you* want an intervention.

66. RAILROADED

There's a type of story structure in interactive fiction (IF) and video games that's known as a "railroaded" story. You may be offered some choices, but the choices are fake; no matter what you do, you're "railroaded" onto the same fixed storyline. Game designers do this because creating meaningful choice in an interactive narrative is expensive in terms of work. (I've seen some procedural plot generation but as I write this, that tends to have its own quirks and pitfalls.)

Stephen Bond's IF game *Rameses* uses railroading to brilliant effect in characterizing its dysfunctional, disaffected hero, a boy at an Irish boarding school. Basically any time you try to get the hero to *do* anything, he point-blank refuses because he's too depressed/apathetic. There's a sense in which the game isn't interactive, because you can't affect the way the plot plays out. Some players found this frustrating, but it works thematically as a commentary on the hero's psyche.

The ideal of a complete sandbox game where the player can do *anything* has yet to be realized in video game format; you're probably better off sticking with tabletop games mediated by a human group or a gamemaster(s). But video games do occasionally use *limited* choice to good effect.

One such example is the sci-fi/survival phone game *Lifeline*, in which you play someone giving advice over the radio to a ship-wrecked student, Taylor, trying to survive on a hostile planet. Every time Taylor checks in and asks you what to do, you can only choose between two responses. That's it! But that plus a bunch of bifurcating choices lead to a number of possible outcomes.

Sometimes when we're writing a story in static (non-interactive) format, we get overwhelmed by the idea that *anything could happen*; by the infinite multiplicity of options. *Railroading* yourself as such doesn't work, in that if you already knew what you wanted to happen next you'd be writing it. But sometimes it's helpful to narrow things down to Just Two Options. Then you can think through the options and their implications, and pick the one that works better for the story you want to tell, so that you can break the logjam.

So maybe your cat-girl thief owes money to a loan shark. Two choices: skip town (you're bored of the current city anyway) or take on a risky job stealing antique spellbooks (which lets you show off her 1337 skills).

Or maybe your space pirate can't decide who to take as their plus-one to the Space Pirate Convocation. Two choices: their loyal but taciturn first mate, who's been with them through thick and thin, or the planetary princess they kidnapped for the ransom but are falling for.

Or maybe your master spy's cover has been blown at a banquet. Two choices: fight his way out past the chained demons or take his "best friend," who's sitting next to him, hostage.

Narrow it down to Two Options, without worrying about "best options," and then pick one of them.

67. WANTED POSTER

As kids, my sister and I came across a fun illustrated storybook that told the tale of a bandit outwitting the sheriff et alia in a Wild West tale. It was customizable in the sense that the bandit's face was left blank and you were supposed to paste a headshot in so that *you* could play the role of the clever bandit. We never actually did this because we were worried about "ruining" the book, but we loved the conceit.

I'm an "omniscient" thinker. I have a hard time separating out what character A thinks about character B and vice versa unless I explicitly make some kind of chart with that information—and even then I'll probably forget to look at it while writing. The d10 edition of the roleplaying game Legend of the Five Rings had a really neat thing with its varied clans that showed what each clan thought about all the other clans; these were not necessarily symmetric!

One thing you can do in this situation is to make wanted posters for your characters. What does the antagonist think is the most tactically important information about the protagonist, or vice versa? Liven this up with art from whatever source for personal use, vital statistics, descriptions of fighting style, places they're likely to hang out, the reward for anyone who calls in a tip!

68. FILK

Filk music seems to be a love-it-or-hate-it affair. I was introduced to it in middle school via what was almost certainly an illegal cassette copy of a bunch of Star Trek filk songs, and then I mail-ordered some tapes of ballads based on Mercedes Lackey's Valdemar and Tarma & Kethry books/stories. (I realize that by referencing cassette tapes I am showing my age. I remember when *computers* ran off tape drives. Of course, my mom remembers programming with punch cards in college. But I digress.)

I vividly remember one of the Tarma & Kethry mercenary stories that contrasted the "ballad" version of a job they did, composed by an annoying bard, with the very, very different real version of what actually happened. A friend informs me this is "Threes" by the filk singer Leslie Fish, or "Leslac the Bard."

In any case, stuck on plot? Wondering what the right next move is for your characters? Throw all that out and instead write a *filk song* about what happens! Play everything up for humor or melodrama or cheesy puns or rhyme! *After* you have your filk song, you can work backward to what "really" happened.

By the way, my secret weapon for things like this is the rhyming dictionary—I use an app, but you can find ones online if you Google.

Here's what happens when my space general/mass murderer Jedao's backstory from the Machineries of Empire series turns into a country song:

> I was just another rookie with dead-eyed aim
> Fell into the orbit of a fox-eyed dame
> Joined the army, where I never lost a fight
> The wars and the conquests never felt right
>
> I learned to treat my life like a tournament of chess
> I planned a revolution with no hope of success
> Just as well math was the only subject that I failed
> I wasn't going to stop until a new order prevailed

...I could go on, but that would be cruel and unusual. Now it's your turn!

69. MIRROR, MIRROR

I am not a historian of tropes so I have no idea who popularized the "Mirror universe where there are evil versions of your heroes" if it wasn't original Star Trek's "Mirror, Mirror." Probably it goes back to "evil twin" narratives all over the world that predate written language. Personally, I was in middle school when I saw that Trek episode and I almost failed to cope with Evil Spock having a beard.

(I hope this doesn't count as a spoiler, the way that it's impossible to spoil Ira Levin's *The Stepford Wives* these days. Or Shakespeare, for that matter.)

If one of your heroes was replaced by the mirror evil version of themselves, how long would the evil version be able to keep up the act? (Yes, I am thinking of a certain TV show I really enjoyed and failing to name it because, well, spoilers.) Who would suss them out? Who *wouldn't*?

Or if one of the villains was replaced by the *good* version of themselves, how would they navigate this situation?

What if a character was replaced by a mirror self *and no one could tell?*

One of my favorite things in fiction is that moment when a

protagonist character is one bad decision away from becoming just like the villain. Thought exercises like this one help me think of juicy scenarios for those moments.

70. LILACS AND OTHER SINS

If you have scent or chemical sensitivities, maybe give this one a miss. My sister is allergic to certain common perfume ingredients so needless to say my perfumes take a vacation when she visits me or vice versa! (My husband and daughter have no sensitivities, and my cat shows no sign of reactions, either.)

I don't have an unusually good sense of smell, but I have *some*. I love the fragrances of flowers, and some of my happiest memories are of the scent of the first lilacs of spring, back when I lived in South Korea. I have not sniffed lilacs in over a decade; they don't seem to grow in Louisiana where I currently live, and I've never managed to visit a place that has them during the time of year when they bloom.

Still, I get my dose of flowery scent during the long growing season in Louisiana. One of the houses in the neighborhood has jasmine, and I love its fragrance when I go for nighttime walks. My thing lately has been planting roses that have an odor. My house came with two well-established and gorgeous rose bushes, but *none of the roses has a fragrance*. So far I've planted a Marie Pavié, which smells vaguely similar to lilacs; a Dame de Coeur, which also had a lilac-like smell; a Chrysler Imperial, which smelled of *citrus*; a Femme Fatale, which smells like a classical rose; and a 1000 Wishes, which theoretically has a rose-like fragrance but is very faint unless you get to the blossoms in the morning *just* after they bloom for the first time.

My husband, on the other hand, has an unusually *poor* sense of smell. For years I wondered why he kept annoying me by forcing me to sniff every single refrigerator item (chicken, beef, milk, cheddar, whatever) in order to check whether it had spoiled yet or not. I finally snapped at him and that was when I found out that he literally can't smell the difference between spoiled and still-good versions of these foods, so he has to rely on me. (Well, and cheese is a problem anyway in that cheese is *inherently* odoriferous, heh.) It had never occurred to me that his sense of smell could be that bad, and it had never occurred to him that I needed to be told.

Smell is important to me and I often use perfumes for inspiration. I often associate characters with perfumes. I've long been a fan of Black Phoenix Alchemy Lab's (BPAL) perfumes, but I also use perfumes from other places. For me, for instance, my traitorous general Jedao will always be Haus of Gloi's Smoked Chai; the villainous immortal mad scientist Kujen is BPAL's Harvest Moon 2006, which on me smells like apples and wheat and bonfire smoke; my YA heroine Hwa Young, who is themed around winter/ice, is BPAL's Pediophobia (it means "fear of dolls"), which my friend Stephanie introduced me to, and which is a sort of chilly austere vanilla/cognac/dust smell that really encapsulates the character for me.

Mostly, I think it can be fun to be open to *all* the senses when we think about our characters—not just their appearances, but smells that make us think of them, or textures (prickly? snuggly? soft?). Also it gives me an excuse to proliferate my perfume collection, so there's that.

71. MEPHISTOPHELES

I am afraid that my introduction to the character of Mephistopheles came about not due to a lifelong learner interest in German folklore or literature (although these are indeed very interesting!), but because we Gifted & Talented kids in middle school loved to try to show each other up with long, hard-to-spell words. I still remember that one week in 6th grade when the *students* in GT English were allowed to come up with the vocabulary list for the weekly quiz (as opposed to the teacher). We raced to our dictionaries to find the longest, hardest words possible to torment each other with. (This was in the days before the internet, so we had to use paper dictionaries.) I can still spell antidisestablishmentarianism and pneumonoultramicroscopicsilicovolcanoconiosis from a cold start, even if I barely remember anything else we learned that year. Anyway, that's how I learned about Mephistopheles, Faust's devil.

What is the devil's bargain that *your* character would make for the desire of their heart? Perhaps your soldier is so desperate for revolution that he's willing to commit mass murder. (Hi, Jedao!) Perhaps your bodyguard wants to save her princess from a disastrous alliance so much that she gets in bed (literally or otherwise) with the thieves' guild. Perhaps your lovelorn hero has no choice but gladiatorial fighting to earn the money to impress their lady's parents.

If a devil is too mean, you can go with a genie instead. What people think about your orc barbarian and what the orc barbarian really wishes for himself might be completely different! For example, "owner and chef of a five-star restaurant in the world's biggest city" isn't usually what comes to mind when people say "orc barbarian," but maybe he's secretly an epicure who wants to settle down!

72. LIAR, LIAR

One of the things I had to do when I wrote my debut novel *Ninefox Gambit* was dealing with the antagonist, a ghost who lies like a rug. (My writer/mathematician/poet friend Ursula Whitcher likes the phrase "lies like a skunk," which is even better, although I first heard it from her as an adult—the version I grew up with was "lies like a rug.") This ghost spends the entire book doing his damndest to corrupt and turn the heroine.

In order for the characters' interactions to work, I had to know *every time* the ghost opened his mouth whether he was lying, whether he was telling the truth, and what the truth actually was. For some of you, especially if you are a character-oriented writer, this probably comes naturally. I had to consciously think about it and remind myself to keep track.

One of the things I learned in math class and computer science were Boolean variables and truth tables. (I have a B.A. in math. No one's perfect.) If you hate math, I'll spare you the gruesome bits, but the basic idea of a Boolean variable is that it can either be TRUE or FALSE. No in-between.

Of course, life is rarely that simple. So you might have your character say something that is KINDA FALSE or MOSTLY TRUE instead of 100% TRUE or 100% FALSE. (Yes, mathematicians have a way to handle this. Look up "fuzzy logic"/"multivalent logic.")

If you're stuck on what a character is going to do next, or have happen to them, or their motivation make a list of (important?) statements they have said to other characters. Then go through and give a truth value to each of those statements. Anything from TRUE to MOSTLY TRUE to KINDA FALSE to FALSE, or however it feels comfortable for you.

Now pick one of those statements at random (or purposely, you do you) and flip the truth value. TRUE becomes FALSE. FALSE becomes TRUE. MOSTLY TRUE becomes KINDA FALSE, or whatever feels right to you. (You're not taking a math class. No one's going to grade you for your judgment or your terminology.)

How does this change what your character is going to do, or what their motivations are? What's going to happen to your character? How other characters relate to them?

For example, maybe your psychic investigator told a suspect for murder, "I don't know if you did it" and you originally had this down as a TRUE statement. Flip it and it becomes FALSE. Now the investigator *did* know the suspect committed the murder (or not)...and is lying to the suspect about it. How does that change the story? Does it get you unstuck? If not, does it help to repeat the process with another statement?

If your soul is screaming *no no no this doesn't work* then you can always do the equivalent of hitting undo. But it might help you figure out what *does* work!

73. SPECIFICITY DYE

I'm afraid that World Literature IBH in high school was not one of my favorite classes, 90% of which I attribute to Thomas Hardy's *Tess of the d'Urbervilles*. (I liked Tess fine. I was infuriated by her fate and by the men in her life.) It wasn't all bad; that was also the class that introduced me to Archibald MacLeish's *J.B.* and Joseph Heller's *Catch-22*, although I didn't go on to take any literature courses in college. But there is one *writing craft* thing that the teacher, Mr. Byrd, hammered into our heads that I took as gospel, and that has served me well ever since.

The idea is that of *specificity*. A single sharp, well-chosen detail, Mr. Byrd told us, does ever so much more to conjure a specific image or character or setting for the reader than a paragraph of bland generalities.

For example, take this description:

She had black hair and green eyes. She was pretty tall and she intimidated me.

Bland. Forgettable. (Unless, of course, you're *deliberately* using a plain style, which can be a thing!) Let's gussy it up a bit, fantasy-style:

She had hair that exact shade of a mirror in an unlit room, and eyes that reminded me of crushed moss. She was unfashionably tall, with the presence of a newly sharpened knife.

Let's change the implied setting and the tone:

She had tar-black hair and eyes the color of broken beer bottles. She was tall enough you had to tip your head back to say howdy to her. Just being around her made my bones clatter.

(I'm from Texas, what can I say.)

But it's more words, you say. Well, yes: a few more words up-front, but the impression lingers that much longer. The words have more impact. You could get away with maybe a single line about a character and give more of an impression than "black hair, green eyes, pretty tall," and going on in that particular bland vein for three paragraphs.

I found a similar concept in a book on songwriting, interestingly enough, Pat Pattison's *Writing Better Lyrics*. He describes it as "dripping dye." Basically, if you have a four-line stanza, and you have two "blander" lines and two lines with really specific imagery, you put the specific imagery *first* and the specificity "drips" downward like a waterfall to "color" the later, blander lines.

You can take advantage of this in writing, too! While writing with very specific, colorful imagery and language throughout the entire book can be a thing, I am personally lazy and that takes effort. If you're trying to economize on effort, you can (for instance) give one or two specific details in more elaborate or colorful language, then use more general language in the rest of the paragraph, secure in the knowledge that the specific details have already conjured up a vivid image for your reader.

The other way this is useful is in signposting what's more/less important. I learned this when I was writing text adventures, which have locations colloquially known as "rooms" although they may not be literal architectural rooms. If you have (say) a bathroom in such a game where the toilet and sink are described in loving detail, the player may well expect to be able to interact with them, or that the toilet is (eww) a key to some puzzle. On the other hand, if the bathroom's description is "Just an ordinary bathroom, nothing interesting here," then the player knows to move along. I imagine mystery writers can play with this to plant red herrings and false clues!

74. SUN TZU FOR EVERYONE

I first became interested in military history during 3rd grade, when one of the books we read was about a page or squire and knighthood. During childhood my interest was mostly in classical and medieval warfare. (I read all of Tacitus—in translation—sitting in my high school library, because why wouldn't I?)

Nevertheless, in the interests of a broader education, while I was a sixth grader roaming the shelves of the public library in Houston (Belle Sherman Kendall Branch), I encountered Sun Tzu's *The Art of War* at an impressionable age. The idea that if you get to the "fighting a war" bit then you've already missed out on the most favorable outcome—resolving the conflict by not fighting at all, preferably using trickery—really stuck with me, even though I went on to write military sf books where the most favorable outcome was long gone.

Sun Tzu contrasted interestingly with Miyamoto Musashi's *The Book of Five Rings*, which I also read in 6th grade. Later I ended up reading other books on the topic, like an abridged translation of Vegetius' *De Re Militari* (a source to be treated with caution, I am given to understand), Caesar's *Gallic Wars*, James F. Dunnigan & Alfred A. Nofi's *Victory and Deceit: Dirty Tricks at War*, Ardant du Picq's *Battle Studies* (also in translation)...the list could go on.

If you're writing military sf or an allied genre, what would a military manual by your character look like? How much would they reveal about their philosophy of war?

If you're writing a different genre, you can still use this basic idea. Maybe the courtesan would write an anonymous manual on how to manipulate their clients. Maybe the farm girl turned revolutionary would write an almanac to help people predict the weather. Maybe the pastry chef is the first in his city to write a cookbook with measurements!

75. ORCHESTRATION

One project I completed last year was composing/producing a full-length soundtrack album for my Machineries of Empire series, Banner the Deuce of Gears. I had themes and motifs in mind for various characters and events, but when it came to one particular villain, I was stuck for inspiration. (She ended up not making it into the album. Maybe next time?)

The villain in question is a femme fatale, and I wasn't sure what instrument to assign her. Most of the time this comes to me quickly. One trickster/tactician/villain character is an oboe; a relative of his, younger and brasher, is a trumpet. The two mathematicians are harpsichords because I've always associated the intricacy of Baroque harpsichord music with math. A particular melancholy general turned out to be a concert flute. But what is the correct instrument for a femme fatale?

Because all knowledge is contained in the internet, I resorted to polling people on my Dreamwidth blog as to two questions, restricting the scope to Western music because that's what I write: (a) what is the most (stereotypically) feminine instrument and (b) what is the most *femme fatale* instrument? I had confessed that I thought of classical guitar as a *seductive* instrument but also that it's "masculine" in my head for the (coincidental?) reason that my two instructors in the instrument were both male; one of them had even studied and performed in Spain.

I was surprised by the firestorm of comments touched off, and also by how quickly that tiny subset of the internet, as represented by people who read/vote/comment on my DW blog, converged to an answer. First, the two most "feminine" instruments were (a) concert flute and (b) harp. But people agreed that neither of those were *femme fatale*—for that, people suggested, I might want something like an alto saxophone or perhaps a violin in a certain style.

Some people took umbrage at the notion that a female character should be scored to "feminine" instruments like the flute. The example I gave by way of counterargument, because this is a fallen world, was this: you know Belle from Disney's *Beauty and the Beast*? If Disney hired me to write a theme for her (never happen, but for the sake of discussion), and I scored her to *tuba*, I would be fired on the spot. For better or worse, these instruments and their timbres do have specific character and personality associations, and composers ignore them at their peril.

You may or may not be a composer, but all of this is the long way around to this particular exercise: if you were writing music for your characters, what instruments would each one be? You needn't limit yourself to instruments from classical music. What about electric guitar, or chord zither, or harmonica? Someone suggested one of my characters, a trickster with a quirky sense of humor, should really be a kazoo...

76. SPOILERS!

I don't care whether you prefer to read/watch/etc. things unspoiled or whether you seek out spoilers; you do you. Personally, most of the time I ask to experience things unspoiled, especially if it's TV I'm going to be watching with my husband, because we like to play something we call "plot chess," where we try to predict any twists. We managed to call the twist to *The Good Place* S1 by episode three, but I think the prize here is a friend who figured it out in episode *one* thanks to certain symbolism. My husband is very annoying to play plot chess against because he picks up on clues very quickly, especially if there's a logical framework involved. (He's a physicist. He comes by this honestly.)

On the other hand, sometimes I ask friends about specific spoilers if it's something that I might find difficult to deal with. I skipped *Buffy the Vampire Slayer*'s "Seeing Red" on the advice of my friends and to this day it's the only episode of that show I haven't seen. I often ask whether there's cat harm because that's usually a hard no for me. There was one series of graphic novels that I had to nope out of because it was specifically designed to be unreadable by Yoons: it featured graphic *fox harm* page after page, and I really like foxes.

Spoilers aren't always about upsetting or triggery material. Some-times they're a way to entice me (or others) to join the experience! I once jokingly chided a friend of mine that she hadn't told me that there was *fencing* (the sword kind) in Chung Ha's K-pop music video "Snapping"; that would have gotten me to watch it *instantly*. She replied, "I wanted it to be a surprise!" And learning that *The Wheel of Time* TV show had main lesbian characters got some of my friends to try it out.

If you're stuck for what to do next, try writing a "fake spoilers" guide by one of your characters, or by a hypothetical reader. This could be a fun way to explore upsetting or enticing possibilities. Bonus points if your character has a completely gonzo bizarre idea of what's "traumatic" or "enticing," like jigsaw puzzles or julienning carrots. (I'm sure everyone who's read Tamsyn Muir's *Harrow the Ninth* is now thinking about the cooking!)

77. EXAMS

Some of my early short stories featured exams, probably because I was still a high school or college student at the time I wrote most of said stories. If my editor hadn't given away my age in his comments, I think readers would still have figured it out! Even today I still have nightmares that I haven't done my point-set topology homework and it's due tomorrow. I got a good grade in that class *and* turned in all my homework on time so I consider this enormously unfair!

Recently my daughter, who goes off to college in the fall, had to go through the gauntlet of AP exams. I trolled the poor kid by offering to buy her one of those "everything you need to know about X subject" books...for middle schoolers. She just rolled her eyes. (A common occurrence.)

Not all settings have formal schooling (and for who?) or exams, but there are usually rites of passage. What kinds of exams exist, if relevant? Maybe a world of magic and farming tests people on their ability to sex chicks or predict the weather. Maybe orphans raised as assassins are given a murderous assignment on their thirteenth birthday. Maybe astrogators are trained in the constellations of a thousandfold worlds.

78. CRYPTOLOGY

I've been fascinated by codes and ciphers since childhood, although mainly this started with substitution ciphers and learning Pig Latin. Years later, in college and grad school, I took a couple math courses that were either about cryptology or crypto-adjacent. One of them culminated in the professor giving us photocopies of Rivest, Shamir, and Adleman's "A Method for Obtaining Digital Signatures and Public-Key Cryptosystems" paper—the one that described RSA public-key cryptography. I no longer have the photocopy (flood casualty) but a PDF of the paper resides on my iPad. And for kicks, I used techniques I'd learned for decrypting the Vigenère cipher to crack the "secret message" in Alan Garner's "Tam Lin" retelling *Red Shift*. (I don't recommend using the slow and tedious brute force method I employed; the novel itself gives you a much faster crack.)

You don't need to become an expert in cryptology and cryptosystems to get some use out of this. Indeed, the state of the art changes rapidly and is likely top secret to boot. One of the reasons I ultimately decided not to apply to the NSA for a job was that one of my math professors said he could always tell which mathematicians at conferences worked for the NSA because they hung around the hallways talking about baseball statistics instead of their classified research.

This sounded like a miserable fate. I apologize if you're a baseball fan!

When I'm discussing hopes and fears and plans for some of my works in progress, I often have readers/friends who want to avoid spoilers. At that point I resort to ROT13, a very simple cipher. The point is not that it can't be cracked (indeed, I usually link to that site for easy decryption) but that it protects the casual viewer from being exposed to spoilers. If they *want* to know, they can copy-paste the text into the site and get the cleartext back.

Sometimes when I go back to review my notes or these discussions, I'll come to a dead stop when I run into one of these encrypted segments. The beauty is that I have the memory of a goldfish, so sometimes *I* don't remember the spoilers either. It gives me the freedom to imagine new possibilities. And if I'm still stuck, or I want to compare those imaginings to my original plans, I can go decrypt the notes and find out! It's really the best of both worlds.

79. THE SCRIBE'S WORK

Once upon a time, as a kid in Texas, I was so enamored of Diane Duane's Star Trek tie-in novel *Spock's World*, encountered at the library, that I decided I wanted a copy for myself. It didn't seem to be available in the bookstores of the day, Waldenbooks and B. Dalton and so on, and this was long before Amazon and online booksellers were a thing. Besides, I was in middle school; I barely knew how credit cards worked, and certainly didn't have one of my own.

Innocent of copyright considerations, I undertook to make my own copy by...writing the entire book out by hand on notebook paper. I'm sure this is appalling to you! It's appalling to me in hindsight. If my mom had realized what I was up to she would never have kept topping up my supply of Mead notebook paper!

The endeavor didn't last more than a couple chapters because of writer's cramp. Saved by physical limitations? Even that partial copy no longer exists, thank goodness.

Still, one thing I learned in this ill-advised endeavor was to pay close attention to prose and word choice and phrasing! The lesson would stick with me later when I used to hang around my high school library and copy out favorite poems from collections in the poetry section.

There's something about this sort of forced close reading, where you're obliged to look at every single word in order through the process of copying, that really helps me sharpen my own prose. Consider copying out a favorite paragraph/verse/stanza from a writer or poet or rapper you really admire, and then writing a pastiche in the same style, using what you've learned from your study. You don't have to do this longhand if writing taxes you; use typing or a voice recorder or whatever works for you.

80. SPINNING WHEEL

Have you ever noticed how, when you're installing new software or an OS update on your computer, the "estimated time remaining" is always a lie? I remember one notable instance where I was updating macOS on my laptop and it had said "approximately 15 minutes remaining" for over an hour. To say nothing of all the times my apps slow to a crawl—it's not for nothing that I dread the "spinning beach ball of doom."

Maps, statistics, graphs, and related constructs are often lies. I remember how eye-opening Darrell Huff's *How to Lie with Statistics* was. Granted, because the book was first published in 1954 and inflation is a thing, I also remember being shocked that $25,111/year (for "the average Yaleman, Class of [19]24") was an "impressive" salary. If only that were still true today!

You can get away with all kinds of chicanery by foxing the scales on the x- and y-axes of a graph, or turning a chart upside-down, and so on. But why not fox your graphs—say, on your writing-a-novel progress chart—for your own psychological benefit?

I've totally done that NaNoWriMo thing where you have a little bar that shows what percentage of 50,000 words you've completed. (Alas, I have never won NaNoWriMo, although I have written novels outside of it!) But that little bar assumes that all words/chapters/sections are created equal.

This might be the case for you—or it might not. Still, there are probably some stages of the writing process that "count" for more. For me, I need to know the beginning, middle, and end before I start a story, or there's a high chance it will founder and I will never finish it. So those words are disproportionately important. Why shouldn't my self-made writing progress chart reflect that? Maybe I should allow myself twice as many stickers for those bits, as opposed to the others that are "just" routine writing work.

Data visualization isn't something I'm good at; I normally rely on online widgets or sticker charts. But if you're an Excel guru or someone who's good at that kind of thing, this could be your opportunity to go to town!

81. SHELVE IT IN ANOTHER SECTION

Over a decade ago, I heard of a film trailer scoring contest in which the idea was to take the same video material, but change the *music* in such a way that it also changed the film's implied *genre*. Like, imagine *You've Got Mail* with creepy pizzicatos and atonal murmurs so it appears to be a horror flick. Or *Gattaca* as a rom-com. I was initially skeptical but I remember watching some of the entries and being amazed at how effective the "joke" scores were in changing the genre of the trailer!

If all else fails, and your book is failing to book, try taking segments of it and reconceptualizing it as a story in a completely different genre. Turn your cozy mystery into steampunk, your zombie apocalypse science fiction into a Regency romance, your literary memoir into a thriller. The exercise might clarify for you where you are and aren't deploying the beloved tropes of your chosen genre to best effect, and suggest possibilities for creative play!

ACKNOWLEDGMENTS

Thank you to my trusty beta readers, Stephanie Folse and Ellen Million.

Thank you to Augusta Scarlett for the fabulous cover.

Thank you to Becca Syme and Terry Schott for their coaching.

Thank you to my husband, Joseph Betzwieser; daughter, Arabelle Betzwieser; sister, Yune Kyung Lee; and catten, Cloud, for all their love and patience.

Last but not least, thank you to everyone who's encouraged me on my writing journey!

ABOUT THE AUTHOR

Yoon Ha Lee is the author of the *New York Times* bestselling book *Dragon Pearl*, which won the Mythopoeic Fantasy Award for Children's Literature and the Locus Award for Best Young Adult Book. He is also known for his Machineries of Empire space opera; the first book, *Ninefox Gambit*, won the Locus Award for Best First Novel and was shortlisted for the Hugo, Nebula, and Clarke awards, and the sequels were also Hugo finalists. Yoon Ha's hobbies include art, composing neoclassical music, and destroying readers. He lives in Louisiana with his family and an extremely lazy catten. You can reach him at deuceofgearsart@gmail.com.

🐦 📷

www.ingramcontent.com/pod-product-compliance
Lightning Source LLC
Chambersburg PA
CBHW072031290326
41934CB00024BA/3065